Dear Elizabeth,

With best compliments.

Jeet

PRAISE FOR *CROSSING THE DIVIDE*

"This beautifully written book is a must-read on two fronts: First, it is an amazing story of an iconic leader, sometimes poignant but always inspirational. Second, it contains pragmatic advice gleaned from Jeet's life lessons that both rising and senior leaders will find transformative. Weaving together stories ranging from Jeet's blind math teacher, Kripal Dutt Joshi, to experiences from Kazakhstan to Australia to the Sudan, the book intersperses guidance on wide-ranging topics from safety to diversity & inclusion. This creates a rich tapestry of actions that one can take to be an agent of positive change. Above all, this book is a celebration of the triumph of the human spirit, one that readers will have a hard time putting down."

—S. Shariq Yosufzai, retired President of Global Marketing and
Vice President, Global Diversity, Chevron Corporation

"Jeet has shared some key insights to life and work in this book in a deeply personal and straightforward way. Anyone who reads this book is destined to find it worth the time invested in doing so. On a personal note, Jeet's impact on my life's journey will never be forgotten."

—Bruce Chinn, President, Chevron Oronite

"In this book Jeet S. Bindra takes us on a journey from his humble beginnings in India to the C-suite. Transcending the obstacles that people who are members of a minority group face even today, Bindra describes how he helped influence the evolution of 'The Chevron Way' by creating a sense of belonging for all stakeholders. In reading this book you will come to appreciate the importance of diversity and inclusion as a bedrock to success and how it fundamentally changes the way organizations operate on all fronts, for the better."

—Andrew Faas, author of *From Bully to Bull's Eye:*
Move Your Organization Out of the Line of Fire

"It was an honor working for Jeet when he was president of refining for Chevron. Ten years later I found myself in the same role, drawing on many of the things I observed and learned from him."

—Mike Coyle, President, Manufacturing, Chevron Corporation

"Jeet is a shining example of someone who captured the American Dream but never lost a sense of where he came from, the lessons he learned along the way, and the people who made it all possible. This book is a manuscript of how experiences shape character and value systems which are incredibly rare in today's world of Ferraris and Facebook. A must-read story about a man whom I continue to look up to and admire."

—Bhavesh (Bob) Patel, CEO, LyondellBasell

"Jeet's strong leadership, friendship, and support throughout the many years we worked together at Chevron played a significant role in helping me develop, grow, and ultimately achieve my goal of becoming a senior human resources executive. Thanks, Jeet, for being such a positive influence and role model for so many people."

—Greg Wagner, Vice President (retired), Human Resources, ChevronPhillips Chemical Company

"Jeet has a remarkable story to share from growing up in poverty in India to reaching the highest levels of corporate America. Intertwined with the defining moments in his personal and professional life are practical business principles that have been informed by his varied experiences and core values of honesty, transparency, and respect of all people regardless of race, ethnicity, orientation, or socioeconomic status. These business principles can be applied by professionals or entrepreneurs across industries and also serve as reminders that diverse and inclusive business practices lead to greater success."

—Andrew Noone, Senior Vice President, UBS Financial Services

CROSSING
THE
DIVIDE

CROSSING

THE

DIVIDE

FROM BENARES TO BOARDROOM

JEET S. BINDRA

PACESETTER
PUBLISHING
COMPANY

Published by Pacesetter Publications Company, Seattle

Edited and designed by Girl Friday Productions
www.girlfridayproductions.com

Image credits (cover): Shutterstock/itsmejust (boats);
Shutterstock/Rawpixel.com (boardroom)
Image credits (interior): All photos courtesy of Jeet Bindra except:
p. 6: Donn Dabney / Left Coast Classics, LLC; p. 123: John
Shakespeare / Sydney Morning Herald; p. 136: AP Photo/
Susan Walsh; p. 148: Crystal Hunt / Edison International

ISBN (hardcover): 978-1-7338102-1-0
ISBN (paperback): 978-1-7338102-0-3

LCCN: 2019903197

CROSSING

THE

DIVIDE

To the fond memory of my beloved parents, who sacrificed everything for their children.

To my lovely wife, Jan, who has stood by me for almost fifty years.

To my loving sons, Amby and Shammi; their lovely brides, Jenny and Melissa; and their wonderful children, Lily, Gracie, Kylie, Lucy, and Frankie, who inspire us to be the best we can be every day.

And to our family and many friends, who have enriched our lives in so many ways.

CONTENTS

FOREWORD

Within these pages you will find three tightly interwoven stories. The first is the amazing and inspirational story of one man's journey from a home in India of extremely modest means to a position as one of the senior executives at a Fortune 20 company. You will follow the path of a truant youth who became an exceptional student, gaining admittance into top universities in India and the United States. You will read about the personal strength and resilience necessary to forge a new life in a new country, especially when you arrive with only eight dollars in your pocket. You will meet the humble, but influential, people along the way who saw something in Jeet and offered to mentor, guide, support, and challenge him.

The second is a story of leadership and the unrelenting pursuit of excellence in self and in others that demands the highest levels of performance possible. You will discover the courage required to rise above—in spite of, and in defiance of—systems and individuals posing barriers when you may not "look like us or talk like us." You will learn, by Jeet's examples, that personal integrity is the only way to maintain a steady, internal North Star. You will also learn that honest self-examination may lead to an admission of falling short and owning accountability for your own actions. As you get deeper into his story, you will read about the long-lasting impacts of investing in the professional and personal growth of colleagues and subordinates and the ways in which it is possible to amplify your leadership through a competent and committed organization. Finally, you will realize that taking risks in your career to venture into the unknown is made easier if you are blessed with a spouse who is equally adventurous and courageous.

The third story is one which you, the reader, will be able to write for yourself. Throughout these pages are questions for you to consider as you define or refine your own aspirations, adaptability, self-governance, nonnegotiables, identity, and relationships within all aspects of your life. Jeet invites you to self-reflect, using his own experiences as examples and by offering up the lessons he has learned along the way. He steers clear of a specific template for success; rather, he offers a map with which to evaluate whether your own leadership behaviors are achieving the outcomes you desire, and to make difficult life and career decisions.

I have known Jeet my entire adult life. Here is the story, in his authentic voice, of the trying circumstances under which we met and the persistence with which Jeet reached out to establish a relationship with me. He became my first boss after I graduated from college. Although we only worked together for three months (which I remind him frequently with a good dose of humorous resentment for pursuing his career), we remained close colleagues. During the past several decades, I have watched as his sons grew from children kicking a soccer ball around the backyard under Jeet's coaching, became loving husbands, and graced Jeet and his wife, Jan, with five grandchildren. My husband, daughters, and even my sister consider Jeet and Jan extended family. We traveled with them in India and visited the holiest site for the Sikh religion, the Golden Temple in Amritsar. While there, I came to fully understand the profound generosity which characterizes Jeet's life: a kitchen which feeds fifty thousand people for free each day and where millionaires sit on the floor and eat side by side with those who have very little or nothing. It explained Jeet's fundamental motivation to give back to others out of his own abundance, and his comfort and ease in moving with and among people from widely divergent backgrounds. Jeet writes of the importance of breaking bread with others—in our case this has been in the form of naan, baguettes, ciabatta, pita, and cornbread—in order to forge valued relationships and lasting friendships over a common meal. My first conversation with Jeet was over a meal, and it changed the course of my life; I am extremely grateful for the wonderful and deep friendship that has taken shape over the many years since that first day we met.

May your own life journey be as joyous, rewarding, and surrounded by friends and family as the one you will read about here.

—Jane Doty MacKenzie, former General Manager, Global
Workforce Development, Chevron Corporation

PROLOGUE

I saw it the moment I stepped onto the lot. The day was hot, as most days are in Los Angeles, and heat waves shimmered off the pavement. The sky was a hazy blue. I'd come straight from work, so I was wearing my usual button-down shirt and slacks. My hair was freshly cut and uncovered by the turban I'd worn without fail since I was a boy, for the last twenty-two years of my life.

I'd been thinking about this car for a long time. Where I grew up, this was *the* dream car. Most cars driving on the streets had been rickety Ambassadors or dusty Fiats, but every now and then a foreign diplomat or some powerful, mysterious person would roll through in his Mercedes. Everyone would stop what they were doing to watch, their own awed faces reflected in the car's polished windows. I'd mentioned this a few weeks earlier to my colleague Bob Fujimoto, and he'd told me that there was a used-car dealership called Jama Motors in Hermosa Beach that often carried secondhand Mercedes, just twenty miles or so south on Pacific Highway.

I'd been looking forward to this expedition and, when I arrived, there it was: a 1984 Mercedes 300SD. From across the lot, its shiny surface reflected the sunlight, the gold paint lighting up like discovered treasure. I made my way over to the car, then slowly walked around its perimeter, taking in its length, its clean lines, the flat grill, the windshield and windows meeting to form a rectangular dome. *God, what a beautiful vehicle*, I thought.

A salesman in a beige suit—this was the late 1980s—approached. "Beautiful vehicle, huh?" he said. "Just came to our lot last week. Would you like to see the inside?"

"Of course," I said, nodding.

He unlocked the driver's-side door and opened it for me. I got in, the brown-leather seat squeaking under me as it took my weight. I put my hands on the steering wheel; the Mercedes symbol stared up at me from its center. I closed my eyes for just a second, imagining driving with the windows down, an ocean breeze cooling my face as I sped along.

After a few minutes, I reluctantly stepped out onto the asphalt. "I'll be right back," I told the salesman. "I need to go talk to my wife."

"Sure thing," he said as I started to turn away. "We can make a deal if you pay in cash. You won't have to do all that paperwork for a loan, either."

I drove home carefully in my Toyota Camry, trying not to let the building excitement overtake me. I cautiously pulled into our drive-way, looking around for our boys, Amby and Shammi. They must have been off playing with friends, because the front yard was quiet.

"Jan?" I called as I opened the front door. My wife walked out of the kitchen, drying her hands on a towel. "Jan!" I nearly shouted. Then I cleared my throat and tried to keep my voice level. "Jan, I've just been to the car dealership. There's a Mercedes 300SD there. A gold one!"

Jan didn't need much convincing. Honestly, she couldn't care less about cars. For her, they were simply a means of getting from point A to point B. But she knew just how much *this* particular car meant to me.

"If that's what you want," she said, "go ahead and buy it."

She and I drove back to the dealership. Jan dropped me off, then drove home to take care of dinner.

After a little haggling and a lot of paperwork, the beige-suited salesman handed me the keys. "It's all yours," he said.

I can't really describe the feeling I had driving that car home. Pride, exhilaration, simple joy. I had goose bumps. Palm trees and pedestrians blurred outside the windows as I cruised along, windows down, just like I'd pictured. The noises and smells of the city streamed past me.

That is a moment I will remember forever. Of course, that car is long gone, and other cars have taken its place and then gone, too, as my family and I moved around the world. But that one car, that gold Mercedes 300SD, sticks so vividly in my mind because it wasn't really about the car. It wasn't really about material wealth—although, if you've lived in poverty as I have, you know that material wealth does matter, and I can admit that owning this car, driving this car, being seen in this car was important to me. But more than that, it was about what that car *meant*. It meant that I, a boy who'd grown up with just enough food in his belly and a roof over his head but not much else, had made it. It meant that I could provide for my family, that I could afford nice things not just for myself but for them, too. It meant that I had, and would continue to have, enough to share. It meant I'd be able make the road easier for my children, and many years later, for my grandchildren. It meant I'd be able to build friendships all over the world, friendships based on generosity. It meant I'd be able to take care of my communities, both the ones I'd built in the United States and the one I'd left in India in 1969. It meant that all my hard work, all those early mornings biking to school, the separation from my family and the culture I'd grown up with, the evenings after class spent cooking chicken curry and *aloo gobhi* over a hot stove in India House Restaurant on The Ave in Seattle, the late nights studying, the scraping by on lentils and six hours of sleep—all of that had been worth it.

Rarely, if ever, will you be handed a golden egg, and, in my experience, there's a perpetual shortage of road maps to success. I certainly did not receive such a road map, though I did meet plenty of kind people who were willing to point the way. It is largely because of them that I was able to earn that gold Mercedes and other symbols of success, to climb the corporate ladder both due to *and* despite my background, and to make a beautiful home for my family.

Now that I am retired from the daily grind, I wish to impart the wisdom I've learned over many years of hard work, during the long and sometimes treacherous journey I've taken from the humble place of my birth. I've written this book first for my family and friends, so that they know where I came from, why I worked so hard to achieve, and how important they are to me. I've written with another audience in mind, too: aspiring professionals, in particular those who will have to transcend the obstacles created by people who underestimate them. I have also captured many lessons that may resonate with people of varied backgrounds and demographics.

This book will give you the methods I've determined, through much trial and error, to be the most effective for breaking down barriers and lifting up not just yourself but those around you. Included are insights around the big-picture perspective and mindset necessary for pursuing your goals, suggestions for building a strong and authentic network in your personal and professional lives, and technical advice on the day-to-day processes of working and leading. I have not shied away from my own mistakes and regrets—the hard lessons I learned through failure informed my accomplishments as much as, if not more than, the achievements more easily reached. If nothing else, my wish is that you remember and feel empowered by this: it is up to you to make your own breaks.

CHAPTER 1

DREAM THE IMPOSSIBLE DREAM

I was born in Benares (now known as Varanasi), a holy city on the west bank of the river Ganges. For thousands of years, Aryan settlers, Buddhist pilgrims, Muslims conquerors, and British colonizers have lived in and visited my hometown in north central India. It is a place of shrines and temples and ashrams right on the water's edge, of winding stone alleys and wandering cows, loud markets and red sunsets. Every year, millions of Hindus walk along the road known as Panchakosi to the Ghats, the long steps that lead down to the water, where they bathe and spread the ashes of loved ones. On any given day, you can see smoking funeral pyres, groups of women doing their laundry, livestock cooling off, and someone performing a religious ritual, all next to one another by the flowing water.

My birthday came a little over one month after Independence Day, when India reclaimed its sovereignty from the United Kingdom in 1947. Of course, I have no memory of those volatile days and months after, as people tried to navigate the new borders, the drawing of which led to an outbreak of violence and mass displacement. I imagine my parents, as Sikhs, were worried about the struggles of their fellow minority members to the northwest, on either side of the newly created

Pakistan-India border. Perhaps my older sister, Jaswant Bahan Jee, and my older brother, Baljeet Veer Jee, have some hazy recollections of this time. They would have been six and three, respectively. My younger siblings, brother Manjeet and sister Navneet, would arrive a few years later, in 1949 and 1954 respectively. Per Sikh tradition, my brothers, my father, and I had all been given the middle name "Singh," and my sisters and mother had all been given the middle name "Kaur." Together, the seven of us lived in a small house. Our water buffalo, Sundari—meaning "beautiful" in Hindi—lived under a tree out front, and every day we'd mix mustard cake with chopped corn or wheat stocks to feed her. In return, she would give us milk, part of which we sold and part of which my mother turned into yogurt, buttermilk, and ghee for the family. Our dozen or so chickens lived in a pen nearby.

My first real memories involve climbing trees and playing soccer barefoot in the shadows between houses or in empty fields under a hot afternoon sun. I remember, too, getting into fights, something I developed a reputation for early on, as well as very much *not* wanting to go to school. My family could afford just enough vegetables, chapatis (Indian bread-like tortillas), and beans to stave off the hunger of five growing kids, and still my mother found a way to try to entice me. This is how much she and my father cared about their children's education. "Jagjeet," she'd say, "what special food can I make you for lunch to take with you to school?"

"Sweet paratha," I'd reply, knowing full well that, once I had my treat in hand, I'd walk toward the school until I was out of sight, then climb a tree and eat it before running off to play.

My father—who worked as a supervising electrician for the Military Engineer Services, a civilian branch of the army—soon realized that my mother's attempts at bribery were failing, and so he tried other measures. First, he tried reasoning with me, then yelling at me, and then threatening to lock me in the small wood and coal shed behind the house, where a nest of mice had made a home. When the threats didn't work, what else could he do but follow through?

It was pitch-black in that shed, and it smelled of dust and cobwebs and old animal droppings. I could hear the soft scrape of little mice feet near my head.

"You're not coming out until you promise to go to school," my father said.

When I think about my life and about all the things that fell into place to allow me to become what I have become, I trace my trajectory back to that musty shed. This might sound strange, I realize, especially given that such a style of parenting might not go over so well these days. I never locked my own children in a shed, or slapped them for that matter, and I would not advocate for anyone else to do so, either. Yet my father's action, which would be viewed as extreme in American culture today, did alter the course of my life. It didn't take me long in the musty dark to make that promise, one which I managed to keep because, once I started going to school, I realized that I had a knack for it. I surprised everyone by no longer needing bribes or threats—being good at something was reinforcement enough. Soon I began to look forward to going to school at Cantonment Junior High School in Allahabad Cantonment, built by the British to serve as a military residence. My classmates and I would roll out jute mats and sit on the floor, a slate and chalk in hand, or some paper, an ink pot, and a *kalam*—a stick of bamboo with the end sliced off at a diagonal to make a writing nib.

My afternoons were free for climbing trees and getting up to mischief, and often my friends and I would walk over to the military residence's tennis courts, where young officers dressed neatly in white played the game. We would stand at the fence, our eyes moving back and forth to follow the trajectory of the ball, the only sounds the thwack of it hitting the rackets and an occasional grunt from one of the players. We didn't care about the game itself—I much preferred soccer—but we hoped that the officers would take pity on us and throw a tennis ball our way. I also took this time to observe the officers: how tidy their clothing and how clean their canvas shoes were, how healthy and confident they seemed. I wouldn't have been able to articulate it at the time or understand the reasons why, but I had a sense that I wanted to be on the other side of the fence.

Every now and then, one of the young men would wipe the sweat from his brow and then, nonchalantly, lob the ball over to us. We'd race to grab it, then run off to play soccer, kicking the tennis ball with our bare feet.

As I finished my time in primary school, my older brother, Baljeet, was finishing the eighth grade. He would be going to a new school the following year. My father, always looking for ways to organize his big family and consolidate his spending, said, "Why don't we enroll you both in the same school so that you can use one bike?"

To get to City Anglo-Vernacular Intercollege in Allahabad, Baljeet pedaled while I sat on the handlebars. We arrived very early in the morning—the school couldn't accommodate the large population of children in the area, and so we attended in shifts. Baljeet and I were on the first shift, which began at 6:30 a.m. and ended at 11:30 a.m. My first experience sitting at a desk was at City Anglo-Vernacular Intercollege. I had other firsts there as well: I truly had to try in order to keep up with my peers, and I felt a spark of competitiveness—previously, I hadn't really had to work in order to prove myself. Now I would have to hit the books if I wanted to stay ahead. At this point in my life, I was the one holding the highest standards for myself, though my parents continued to encourage and celebrate my accomplishments every step of the way. But it was my inner drive that propelled me to succeed, to get the highest grades I possibly could—second best wasn't good enough.

Those years went by fast, with morning bikes with Baljeet to school and study sessions late into the evenings. As the end of my ninth-grade year approached, my father was transferred to Ranikhet, a town to the north known for its stunning views of the Himalayas. It, too, had been established in the mid-1800s as a military residence by the British, prized because the weather was cooler than the cities to the south.

I can't say that I was overjoyed about the move. I'd established a rhythm to my days, a reputation for excellence, and friendships that I was sorry to lose. I was even sorrier to discover that my new school, National Higher Secondary School, Ranikhet, used a different set of books than my previous school, a set with which I was completely unfamiliar. Not only that, but I, along with all tenth graders, would be taking the statewide exam for admittance to intermediate school at the end of the year. I imagined with dread the day of the exam, could see in my mind's eye the other students' relaxed faces next to my scowling one and their pencils flying over the test pages as I slowly scratched along. With this trial looming, I approached my father.

"How am I going to catch up, Papa Jee?" I asked, bemoaning my fate. My father paused. I'm sure he was doing some kind of mental calculation—adding up the cost of running a household, feeding a family, and all the other big and small expenses—and searching for some slender margin that could be put toward my education. I tried not to fidget as I waited for my father's mental wheels to stop turning, for him to hand down his verdict. I trusted him; he would find a way to help me.

Later, when my father retired in 1969, he was making less than one hundred dollars a month. That was chicken feed even in those days. Yet I never felt poor, because all our neighbors were poor as well. When everyone else is in the same boat, you don't realize what you're missing. My siblings and I didn't always have soccer shoes or a real soccer ball to kick around, but when it came to schooling, my parents always found a way. I don't know what corners my father cut, what sacrifices he and my mother made. I suppose children rarely do.

The afternoon after my father announced that he'd found me a tutor, I followed his directions to the home of the Joshi family. Now, most kids might not be thrilled with the prospect of having to go to more school *after* school. But if there was one thing I hated it was falling behind my peers, and fantasies of failure fueled my anxiety. The Joshis' house was located three-quarters of a mile from mine, about a quarter mile before the school. I walked past younger children racing down the sidewalks and women hanging laundry from clotheslines above my head. I knocked on the door.

"Come in," a voice called from inside.

I opened the door and stepped inside. It took a moment for my eyes to adjust from the bright light outside to the dimness within. After a moment I saw a single room with a hard-packed dirt floor and small squares cut out of the wooden walls to let in a little bit of light. Two men stood on either side of an old man, who sat on a mat on the ground. "Come," he said, "sit down here across from me." It wasn't until I'd placed my schoolbag down and was seated that I noticed the tilt of his head, the fact that his eyes weren't tracking my movements.

"Hello," I said formally, my hands folded in a respectful greeting, though he couldn't see me. I would find out later that Shri Joshi had lost his eyesight many years earlier, in his forties, from macular degeneration, a genetic disease that was also encroaching upon the vision of his two sons.

"Hello, Jagjeet. I am Kripal Dutt Joshi," he said. "I will be teaching you math. Harish, my eldest son, will be teaching English, and Satish, my second son, will be teaching you Hindi."

Within a month, they'd taken me under their wings. As the family patriarch slowly lost his vision, he had set about memorizing the entire math book, cover to cover. "Jagjeet," he'd say, his hands empty and his eyes unfocused, "turn to page 247, question four." Every time, this filled me with awe. An entire book, memorized! I'd had no idea that memory was like a knife that could be sharpened, a muscle that could be strengthened, a container that could grow to fit the size of its contents. Later, when I was making it a point to always memorize the names of my hundreds of colleagues and employees—as well as many of their significant others and children—I would think back on these moments with Shri Joshi, whom I called Bade Master Sahib, a term of respect reserved for one's elders. If he could memorize an entire math book and more, surely I could memorize the names of those with whom I worked.

Now, instead of my mother having to bribe me to study, in the evenings she'd have to close my book and push me out the door, saying, "Go meet your friends." Otherwise I'd spend all night pouring over math and science problems and English sentences.

By the end of tenth grade, I was more than caught up and more than ready to take the statewide exam, along with the other several hundred thousand tenth graders. I was nervous, of course, and determined to prove myself, but I also felt sure in the fact that I'd done everything I could to prepare.

"How did it go?" my mom asked when I got home after the test, late in the afternoon.

I shrugged, as teenagers do. "OK," I said, nonchalantly.

We waited for the results, and I did my best to contain my impatience. In those days, the results were announced in the local newspaper, the *Pioneer*, which was published in a city called Lucknow, a ten-hour bus ride away. This meant that those of us in the farther reaches of the vast country were always at least one day behind. I've never been one to wait, and so I started visiting the military telephone exchange, where I could ask my father's friend to call an associate in Lucknow to inquire about the newspaper listing. Finally, after many afternoons of disappointment, this man hung up the phone with a smile.

"You are ranked fifty-second out of the top one hundred in the entire state," he told me.

This meant that I would be awarded a National Merit Scholarship, allowing me to attend Ranikhet Inter College. I ran home as fast as I could to deliver the news, then turned back around and raced to the home of the Joshis.

I worked very hard for the next couple of years, ultimately taking the exam for twelfth graders and again winning a national scholarship. Now, however, I didn't know what to do next.

"You can go to college," one of my teachers told me. "Get a bachelor's degree. There's this new institution called the Indian Institute of Technology. It has a world-class engineering program. Of course, it's very difficult to get into."

I knew a challenge when I heard one.

There is nothing about my past that is all that different from any of millions of hardworking individuals around the world. Of course, I was born at a certain moment in history, to a particular family, inside a particular culture, the same as anyone else. The fact that I grew up with very little by way of material wealth does not make me unique; rather, such limited resources are the rule rather than the exception, whether we're talking about the inner cities of Beijing, the farmlands of Punjab, or even the small towns of rural California. So what is it that set me apart, that launched me beyond the circumstances of my birth? I believe much of the credit can be given to my parents' high esteem for education and their fervent desire to see their children succeed in school. For many immigrants throughout the world, this same value is the key to upward mobility, as it is for anyone who wishes to succeed. It is part of the desire to learn not just about the world but about how to best carve your own small place in it. Here is how you can use that insatiable curiosity in the search for new ideas, new opportunities, and new frontiers.

DREAM THE IMPOSSIBLE DREAM—AND PREPARE FOR THE ADVERSITIES THAT LIE AHEAD

I believe that, no matter how humble your beginnings, it is possible to change your life—if you are willing to devote an incredible amount of blood, sweat, and tears, and if you can think bigger than and beyond your immediate situation. As an adult, I would learn about farmworker and labor leader Cesar Chavez, whom I came to consider a wonderful model of how to dream big.

Born to a family of migrant farm workers who had lost their farm during the Great Depression, Chavez attended more than thirty elementary and middle schools. His formal education ended early, but he possessed an insatiable curiosity and so sought out informal avenues for learning. His dream was to create an organization to protect and serve farmworkers, and despite his humble start and the untold number of obstacles he faced, Chavez went on to found the National Farm Workers Association, which later became the United Farm Workers of America. This organization fought for fair wages, medical coverage, pension benefits, and humane living conditions—just what he'd dreamed it would do.

Life rarely follows the path that we originally charted, but if you have an idea of the destination, you might just find an alternative route. Though, of course, dreams sometimes change, this clarity makes it easier to persevere when obstacles appear. Whatever you do, don't give up and let obstacles get in the way of your success. If you haven't already, ask yourself:

- What is your greatest dream?
- What obstacles have you already faced, and how have you overcome them?
- What are some lessons you've learned that might be helpful to you the next time an obstacle gets in your way?

BE HONEST ABOUT YOUR STRENGTHS AND WEAKNESSES

Recognizing your own deficiencies requires humility, one of the traits I most admire. To get anywhere, you have to be able to see what *inside you* is getting in your way. It is only through knowing your own weaknesses that you can work to become stronger. When I changed schools, the challenge of mastering English and Hindi without formal school support became obvious. Not all deficits will be so easy to spot, and so it is up to you to dig deep, no matter how painful, and acknowledge the truth about yourself. At the same time, having an understanding of your strengths is important, too. Not only will it provide an ego boost after a long day of examining your weaknesses, it will allow you to use your strengths to their fullest and develop them further. Ask yourself:

- What feedback have you received from trusted sources about areas in which you might improve? About areas in which you already excel?
- When you look at your career and your life, where do you see patterns of failure? Where within those patterns does your responsibility lie?
- What are your greatest strengths? What can you do to build upon them?

BROADEN YOUR NETWORK TO FIND MENTORS

The Joshis provided my first experience of real mentorship. Their model of dedication, and the way in which they were committed to learning, no matter their limitations, pushed my motives past basic competitiveness toward a real desire to learn and grow. It was obvious just how passionate these men were about what they did, and I couldn't help but internalize that same passion.

The Joshis weren't the only mentors that got me where I am today. I'd soon meet a professor who set the bar high, and then even higher, while giving me the motivation and support I needed to reach it.

The development of the Indian Institute of Technology (IIT) began in 1951 as a joint project between the Indian government and the British government, with support from the United States, West Germany, and the Soviet Union. To get into these prestigious institutions, I would have to take the Joint Entrance Exam. Out of around three hundred thousand aspiring students, the school would only take 1,500, three hundred for each of the five campuses.

"You might not get in," my father said. "Why don't you sit for the National Defense Academy exam, too?"

I agreed; though I was determined to get in, I was pragmatic, too.

I didn't have to think twice about where I wanted to go when I heard that I'd been accepted at IIT. I was good at math and science, and I wanted to push myself harder in these realms to see what I could achieve. Soon I was invited to meet with a group of administrators and faculty at the campus in Kanpur.

"What do you plan to study?" one of them asked.

"Chemical engineering," I said.

He looked at me. "The chemical engineering program in Kanpur is full at this time. We do, however, have space in the civil engineering program."

I didn't say anything. I couldn't afford to go to one of IIT's other campuses in order to start in the chemical engineering program.

"Look," he said after a moment. "All engineering programs share a common curriculum for the first three years. If you are among the top scholars after your third year, you can switch."

There was really no choice—to do what I wanted to do, I'd have to prove myself, over and over again for the next three years. With that, at least, I could claim some control. But there were so many factors working, if not against me, then not exactly in my favor.

That first day on campus was hot, with temperatures hovering around 115 degrees Fahrenheit. My entering class was the institution's third since its founding, and the little saplings that had been planted around the dry 1100-acre campus looked as young and vulnerable as I felt. Like most college kids, this would be my first time living away from home, from my family, from the Joshis, from everyone and everything I knew, among some of the country's most talented, smartest, and hardworking students. Many of them were from society's upper echelons, with the training and confidence that wealth and its associated privileges can provide. The professors were top-notch Indians and visiting Americans—IIT Kanpur was supported by a consortium of nine US universities. I assumed these experts would have little patience for homesickness or worries over finances. They would hold all of us to the highest standards, regardless of our backgrounds.

I moved into the dorm, memorized my student roll number—64097—and took stock of the situation. I had 110 rupees—the equivalent of roughly sixteen dollars—from my scholarship to last the month. I quickly realized how far that *didn't* go, even if my father and older brother managed to send me something from their own thin earnings. To cover tuition, food, and books, I'd need, at a minimum, two hundred rupees a month just to get by.

My faculty advisor, Professor C. N. R. Rao, was one of the most well-known scientists in India. He was, and still is, a brilliant chemistry and research professor, with a list of accomplishments that could intimidate those at the highest levels of his profession, let alone an eager undergraduate. He has written more than fifty books, and there are many people who think that he deserves a Nobel Prize. I went to this busy and important man and said, "I think I'm in trouble. I . . . I need more financial support." This wasn't an easy thing for me to say, and to his credit, Professor Rao didn't bat an eyelash.

In English, he said, "If you get a GPA of 7.5 out of 10 your first semester, I will find some money for you."

It seemed that there would be no end of people raising bars for me to reach. And to this day I am glad they did. Though perhaps it would have been easier to be handed the money—easier still to be born with a silver spoon in my mouth—this way, my academic striving took on the kind of financial complexity of work in the real world. I'd have to earn everything. I'd have to retain pride in where I'd come from while reminding myself that I could, in fact, earn the top grades and compete with those I judged at the time to be way beyond my league.

I ended the semester with a 9.1 GPA. Professor Rao got me an extra one thousand rupees a year. And I'd seen that I could do it—there was no going back from that high bar.

As you move up in your career, it will be of great luck to meet people who set high bars for you along the way. Of course, it will also be up to you to set high bars for yourself—and then figure out how to reach them; that is what the experts call "a plan." Remember, too, that as you go each action has a reaction, each forward motion is the result of building momentum.

When looking for a mentor, focus on finding a guide, not a guru. Someone who has all the answers ready for you is likely to lead you astray, but someone who listens to your concerns and withholds snap judgement, who respects your intelligence and intuition, and who offers thoughtful advice has a greater chance of empowering you to find your own solutions. A mentor can be a teacher or a colleague, though I would recommend that, when you are further along in your career, you find someone who is not a direct supervisor. Continue to request and utilize your supervisor's feedback, but cultivate relationships outside the direct line of accountability so that you can get help seeing the bigger picture. This way, your mentor will be in a position to offer you valuable guidance without compromising their own obligations to their organization.

IDENTIFY THE STEPS ... THEN TAKE THEM ONE AT A TIME

When I was in high school, my mother suffered from terrible migraines, and many days I'd come home from school to find her in bed, eyes closed and a *dupatta*—a scarf women wear to cover their hair—tied tight around her head. My older sister was married by that point, my dad was at work, my older brother was living a few hundred miles away. Someone needed to cook dinner, and I embraced the role of chef. My mother would whisper instructions from her bed, one step at a time. "Chop one onion," she'd say and, when I'd completed that task, "now a tomato. A head of cauliflower. Put a splash of oil in the wok." The oil would sizzle as it hit the pan. "Add a teaspoon of turmeric. A teaspoon of cumin. A pinch of salt. Some red chilies." This was how I learned to cook, step by step.

Now, like most college students, my overarching goal was to graduate. But, also like most college students, there were a number of obstacles standing in my way, including financial difficulties and the lack of openings in my desired major. I didn't know how to address these issues, and so I asked for help with identifying solutions and the steps involved. I was lucky to have Professor Rao to help me. He was someone who was willing to go outside his scope of responsibility, and I've come to see that there are many kind people in the world like him. The only way to find them, however, is to ask.

Henry David Thoreau, a visionary whose ideas influenced the two civil-rights giants Mahatma Gandhi and Martin Luther King, Jr., said, "If one advances confidently in the direction of his dreams, and endeavors to live the life which he has imagined, he will meet with a success unexpected in common hours."

Building a career is like climbing a mountain. While your ultimate goal might be to reach the top of Mount Everest, that wouldn't be your first expedition. Instead, you would first set out to master smaller peaks, like Mount Diablo or Mount Shasta. While you might not solve your financial worries in one go or get your dream job right after college, it's up to you to keep on climbing. The lessons learned from each climb will empower you to take on taller, tougher mountains.

ESTABLISH A TRACK RECORD

The first three years at the Indian Institute of Technology were a lot of hard work. I maintained my grades and, by the end of the third year, I requested my major be changed from civil engineering to chemical engineering as planned. By that time, I'd established a track record, and though I continued to hold myself to the highest standards, my teachers had begun to simply assume that my work was A level. One time, I let a friend copy part of a project: I got my usual A; he got a C+. My reputation was such that, I believe, the professors would glance at my work and just give it an A.

This is not to say that you should ever perform at anything less than your best; rather, it's to show that consistent, exemplary performance can carry you far. Always, *always* apply your greatest effort to every-thing you do. Whether you stay with a company for a few years or fif-teen, your reputation—not just your human resources file—will follow you wherever you go. So wouldn't you rather people assume excellence than be surprised by it?

Here's how to establish a track record of excellence:

- Never cut corners. Quality should always trump speed. Though you might hit all your deadlines and get your work done twice as fast as your peers, if your work is sloppy or incomplete, that will be what is remembered.
- Follow through on your commitments. Honestly assess your capabilities, your current workload, and other responsibilities before agreeing to take on a new project.
- If you have a good reason for needing more time, ask for an extension in advance of the deadline, rather than once it has passed.

***

In my fifth and final year, Prime Minister Indira Gandhi visited our cam-pus. To this day, she is the only female prime minister of India, born in Allahabad and educated in Switzerland and at the University of Oxford. Her father, Jawaharlal Nehru, had worked with Mahatma Gandhi and was elected India's first prime minister in 1947, after the country won its independence. Indira Gandhi then carried on the family tradition as a career politician before ascending to prime minister in 1966, just a couple of years earlier. She was at the height of her popularity when she visited IIT, and her presence was a very big deal. As the elected student body leader, I was given the honor of offering a word of thanks at the end of her visit. There's a photo of that moment, which has adorned a wall in every house I've lived in across the globe for the last fifty-odd years. It's of me, very young, wearing a button-down shirt and tie, slacks, and turban, welcoming the prime minister to the campus.

Jeet welcoming Prime Minister Indira Gandhi to the IIT Kanpur campus.

With graduation just around the bend, I had to figure out what to do next. Since IIT Kanpur was a US-sponsored institute, most of the professors held doctorates from the United States. They encouraged me to apply to universities in that distant and foreign land. The policy was that each student could only apply to six schools, the idea being that this would allow fellow IIT graduates to share the schools' spots among themselves. I applied to two stretch schools, two match schools, and two safety schools in the US and Canada.

Professor A. Vasudev, my professor of chemical engineering, wrote my letters of recommendation. He had earned his master's degree from Washington State University and his PhD from the University of Washington. When I went to him with my acceptance letters, he carefully examined each, then pulled one out of the stack. "This one," he said. "Throw the rest away." I took the paper from his hand, looked at it, then looked up. "Yes," he said, a single nod his final answer.

Once I'd nailed down the scholarship, I called my dad to give him the news. "Papa Jee," I said, "I have been accepted to the University of Washington." There was a pause, and I could hear the static on the line.

After a moment, my father cleared his throat. "Congratulations, Jagjeet," he said. "I am so proud of you. That is wonderful news." Another pause. "As you know, I am retiring this year. I will have a pension, but it's not much, and your brother's job doesn't pay well at all. How are you going to go to the US? We can't even afford the cost of an airline ticket."

The air went out of my sails for little more than a millisecond. I was no stranger to financial straits, and I'd grown quite adept at finding ways to scrounge together funds. "We'll find a way," I said.

CHAPTER 2

MOVING INTO A NEW ROLE

It was September of 1969 and I'd convinced one of my uncles to cosign a loan, which just barely covered the airplane ticket. I was on my way to the University of Washington via a four-stop flight from Delhi to Bangkok to Phnom Penh to Tokyo to Honolulu to, finally, Seattle. All in all, the trip took forty-eight hours, and, at my height of over six feet, my best naps were taken on the floor of whatever airport I happened to find myself in. I arrived in the United States like so many immigrants before me: rumpled, tired, and hopeful.

As far as immigrants go, I was one of the lucky ones. True, I didn't have much by way of material possessions, with only one change of clothes and eight dollars to my name. But I wasn't fleeing from danger and I did not have the kind of memories that wake up so many refugees in the night. Rather, I had a good education, a good head on my shoulders, and a family that was not only alive and well but fully supported my decision to move away. It was that lifetime of support that gave me the confidence to travel across a couple of continents and an ocean in order to start a new life. I knew no one in the country to which I was going, and what I did know about Seattle, Washington could have fit on an index card. But instead of feeling lost or alone, I felt full of possibility.

Like all exchange students, I'd been assigned by the university to a host family that had kindly volunteered to house me and show me the ropes for the first week after my arrival. After that, and the foreign student orientation at Camp Waskowitz, I found a place on The Ave and 45th Street, in the heart of the University District. There were eight of us in the house, including seven foreign exchange students and one local white male, sharing Goodwill furniture and a two-burner hot plate that we used to cook our budget meals. I was grateful for my mother's cooking lessons as I prepared my simple dinners of chicken, vegetables, and lentils in this cold, rainy city across the world.

Walking through the university's campus toward my room on The Ave proved to be an enlightening experience. I wasn't as attuned to the cultural signifiers of dress that perhaps an American student might have been, though I did notice those who'd foregone slacks and ties for bell-bottoms and paisley shirts, tidy haircuts for unkempt manes. I quickly became used to the smell of marijuana wafting through the commons and the sight of crowds shouting and waving signs, young couples holding hands or, to my surprise, kissing in public. But I had other things to do than stand around and gawk.

For one, I had to find a job. I'd been awarded a research assistantship in the University of Washington's department of chemical engineering prior to my arrival in Seattle, which paid $342 per month, a sum that wouldn't quite cover all my expenses. My shared room cost fifty-five dollars and, beyond food and other necessities, I had the high cost of books to worry about. India House Restaurant just so happened to be nearby and I found work as a cook there, arriving in time for the dinner rush after I was finished with my daily classes and before returning to the lab.

It was an exciting and confusing time. The War in Vietnam was ramping up, as was student political action on campus. In May of 1970, after the deaths of student protestors at Kent State University, a huge weeklong student protest brought the campus to a standstill. Along with the Student Democratic Society and the Seattle

Liberation Front, the Black Student Union and the United Mexican Americans were pushing for an end to the war and equality at home. Every day there were clashes between the administration and the students, the anti-war protestors and the ROTC. There were strikes and protests and riots, young people full of passion determined to change the world. And there I was in the middle of this storm—an immigrant brand-new to the country, simply trying to keep my head above water. I didn't understand what was going on—I didn't have the context—and I was somewhat oblivious, focused solely on working hard and on finding stolen hours during the weekends. During those times, I'd gather my roommates and friends from the Indian Student Association to set up an old projector and watch Indian movies that reminded us of home.

Everything was happening so fast; I would finish my master's degree in fifteen months. As my graduation day approached, Boeing began a stint of devastating layoffs, and I began putting together my curriculum vitae in preparation for the next phase of my life. (Soon unemployment would hit 13 percent, and Seattle would adopt the famous slogan "Will the last person leaving Seattle—Turn out the lights.") I didn't have a typewriter, not that I'd know how to use one even if I had, and so I looked in the classifieds of the university's newspaper, the *Daily*. There I found the listing, "Will do typing, fifty cents a page." I called the number, and a woman answered the phone. After I told her what I needed help with, she said, "Sure, bring it over and I'll be happy to type that up for you."

"Where do you live?" I asked.

"In West Seattle." At more than ten miles away—and with the limited public transportation available at the time—for a person without a vehicle or a bicycle, West Seattle might as well have been the moon.

"I don't have a car," I said. There was a pause.

"How about this," the woman said. "My stepdaughter works in UW's housing office. Why don't you drop it off with her? Her name's Jan."

The following day, I made my way down to the housing office after class. It was a gray autumn morning, which, I knew from my first experience with a Pacific Northwest winter the previous year, would soon lead to long nights and dark days and seemingly endless ice-cold rain.

Inside the housing office it was warm and dry. A young woman sat behind the counter, typing away on a typewriter.

"Jan?" I said.

I returned a few days later to pick up my CV. "Thank you," I said when Jan handed me the typed-up copy. I turned away and then, on second thought, turned back. "Would you like to get coffee?" I asked.

This, in my mind, was not a date. I hadn't thought much about dating—that's just not something we did back home. But I enjoyed the conversation—I learned that Jan had grown up in the area, was majoring in romance languages and Spanish, had an older brother in the air force—and I did have a good time. Afterward, walking home, I realized that I wanted to see her again.

The next time we met was at a classic American-college house party: a keg of beer, some rock 'n' roll, young people dancing and chatting. Jan introduced me to her good friend Amy Okazaki, whom she knew from Spanish class. After several weeks of these casual meetings, I decided it was time to muster up the courage to ask her out on a real date.

Amy Okazaki Maki, Jeet, and Jan in West Seattle.

I planned an afternoon and evening of it. I'd saved up some money, hoping to experience the city beyond my little enclave in the University District. We started with a ferry ride to Bainbridge Island, then dinner at Tai Tung in Chinatown, followed by a performance of *Hair*—the countercultural musical that was all the rage at the time—at the Moore Theater downtown. I didn't fully understand the plot, but I did enjoy the music. After that night, we continued to explore the University District. I tried my first hamburger at Herfy's Burgers, my first steak at a steakhouse in Ravenna, and my first tacos at Outrageous Taco. Jan and I made a habit of going to Pizza Haven on Wednesdays for the $1.75 all-you-can-eat buffet, and we stopped by Farrell's for an ice-cream cone practically every week.

Later in the summer, Jan went on a trip to Mexico with some friends. Whenever I called my family in India, I was acutely aware of the seconds passing and the cents accumulating on my phone bill. "Everything OK?" we'd ask each other and then, after a couple minutes, hang up. But with Jan far away, I didn't even think about cost as, every day, I dialed the number of the hostel or the friends' homes in which she was staying. I was not happy when that bill arrived, but I can't say that I regret it.

That spring, in 1971, I asked Jan to marry me. "Fine with me," said her dad, an easygoing and open-minded man, after we told him and Jan's stepmother the news.

Now I'd have to muster up the courage to tell *my* parents. They wouldn't have guessed that I was dating in the first place, let alone an American woman. A couple weeks after sending the note telling them the news, I received a six-page reply, the gist of which was: *it won't work out.* My father even went so far as to try and negotiate by offering to allow me to marry a woman outside of my caste, as long as she were Indian, even if she were Muslim—a big concession given the tension that existed between Sikhs and Muslims in India.

I upped the ante by writing an eight-page response, arguing that it *would* work out. Later I learned that my brother Baljeet had argued on my behalf. "If you don't allow him to marry whom he has chosen," he said, "you will lose a son." Finally, after a couple more rounds of back-and-forth, my parents relented. They had one condition, however: I had to have an Indian ceremony. Not that they'd know the difference—no one could afford to make the trip out to Seattle for a wedding. Still, I felt that was the least I could do.

We decided to have two ceremonies, one in the Sikh tradition, and one in the tradition of Jan's family. There was no Sikh temple in the Seattle area at that time, but I knew a doctor who had Guru Granth Sahib, the Sikh holy book, and gathered a group at his house on Sundays for worship. "I'd be happy to help," he said when I asked, "but we need a priest." There was a large population of Sikhs in Vancouver, and so Jan and I drove up to Gurudwara Temple to ask for assistance with Anand Karaj, the wedding ceremony. The priest didn't have a car, so we offered to buy his bus ticket. He agreed.

We were married at the YMCA in the University District on May 23, 1971, in the morning per tradition. Many of the traditional rituals we skipped. There was no family exchange of gifts, no henna or *Sangeet* ceremony, no singing and dancing as part of the baraat procession. But our friends did cook up a feast of samosas and *gulab jamun,* and people from the Sikh community and the foreign exchange student

Lavaan Pherey for Jeet and Jan in Seattle.

community came to celebrate our union. Jan's brother was there, and her grandmother flew in from Illinois to attend. Dr. Rajendar Dev Verma, my good friend and post-doctoral fellow at the University of Washington, stood in as family for me. My parents had given their blessing by way of sending Jan the traditional *salwar kameez*—pink trousers worn under a long pink tunic. I wore a matching pink turban. The priest recited Lavaan Pherey, the four prayers that seal the marriage, as she and I walked around the holy book four times. With that, in the Sikh tradition, we were married.

Jan then changed into a pretty blue dress, and together we drove from the University District to the Fauntleroy Church in West Seattle. There, in front of a grand window overlooking a rhododendron bush in bloom, we were married again.

After a short honeymoon in Tillamook, Oregon, we returned to build our life together. I had finished my thesis on the photochromic properties of 1-hydroxyimidazoles, a family of chemicals that my fellow researchers and I discovered changed color when exposed to direct sunlight. I had spent many hours in the lab studying the mechanism (chemical change) of this phenomenon, as well as the kinetics (rate of change). In subsequent years, other chemicals with similar properties would be used to change the color of eyeglass lenses to provide protection from the sun.

Jan and her stepmother typed up my dissertation, and with that I had earned a master's degree from the University of Washington. With graduation my assistantship ended, and so I set out to find another job. Though the economy in Seattle was tanking, I got a job at a frozen pizza company called Chateau Chef as a quality assurance manager for a brief stint right before the company went under. Walter Wilmoth, one of the owners, was kind enough to find me a job as a short-order cook on the night shift at a restaurant just south of Southcenter off of Interstate 5, which kept my head above water until I got a job at Western Processing Company in Kent. There I was responsible for figuring out how to treat the chemical waste that resulted from the wood recycling treatment process.

It wasn't my dream job, though I did learn a lot and got to spend time in the lab. Jan was working in the office of the Seattle Public Schools.

My parents, meanwhile, had been pressuring us to come to India. They were anxious to see me and, understandably, wanted to meet their new daughter-in-law. So in the late fall of 1971, we gave notice to our landlord and employers and booked tickets to Delhi, India.

Just as we were about to leave, we received a telegram from my father, telling us not to come. Yet another war had broken out between India and Pakistan. That night, Jan and I talked it over. We decided to go, based on three reasons. One: historically, these wars were short, and there was a good chance it would be over by the time we arrived. Two: our tickets were nonrefundable. Three: adventure.

BE ADVENTUROUS

If you want to thrive in your career—and in life—you have to be willing to **go into the unknown**. This applies to business, of course, but it also applies generally to life, too, and to whom you choose to surround yourself with. If you want to share your life with someone, then flexibility, curiosity, and a taste for adventure are worthwhile attributes to look for. If not for the adventurousness of my wife, this would be a different story. Her dating me in the first place attests to her openness. Had she balked at the idea of flying into a war-torn country, I would not have held it against her in the least. But she didn't, and so we went, despite the danger and, for her, all the unknowns. There were many new experiences awaiting her there, and she went into each with inquisitiveness and a sense of fun. Initially we slept on a jute cot, with air raid sirens erupting every so often, and we bathed with a mug dipped in tap water that had been collected in a tub. She met my family and their neighbors and friends, some of who quietly asked me, "What is that on your wife's face?" (They had never seen freckles before.) She received her Sikh name, Swinder, from the priest at the Golden Temple. We traveled around the country, by *tanga*, train, and bus.

While staying with my sister in Mumbai, I visited Professor A. Vasudev—the chemical engineering professor at the Indian Institute of Technology who'd encouraged me to go to the University of Washington—at his office at Fiberglass Pilkington Ltd, a British glass manufacturer. By the end of the day, I had a job offer. Jan could have said no outright, and that would have been perfectly understandable. The possibility of living in India was not even a blip on our radar, after all. Had she said she needed time to think about it, or time to discuss the many pros and cons of such a drastic move, that would have been reasonable, too. But when I came home that day to talk it over, she listened and without hesitation agreed.

This was not the naivete of youth, though I'm sure that was a factor. And it wasn't about Jan simply going along with my whims—though she has an easygoing nature and tends to be soft-spoken, she also displays a strong determination when necessary. I believe, and she has since confirmed, that it was her adventurous nature that made the decision so easy, and it was her adventurousness that carried us through as, much later, we moved every two or three years to locales as far flung as Australia and Wyoming as my career developed. Because we both had the adventurer's mindset, we made it work.

From Fiberglass Pilkington Ltd, in Mumbai, I eventually moved on to the position of laundry manager at Taj Mahal Palace Hotel, where I went on my first business trips to New York, London, Vienna, and Rome. Jan managed our household and began a Hindi correspondence course. When my parents visited, she practiced Indian cooking with my father, earning a special place in their hearts. (When her father and stepmother came to visit, her dad learned a hard lesson about the "Western" meal's level of spiciness.) After a year or so, I took a step up the career ladder by getting a job as general manager of operations at Snowhite Engineers Pvt Ltd, a New Delhi-based company that manufactured laundry and dry-cleaning equipment, and so we moved again.

Amby Jeet Bindra was born in October of 1975 at the Talwar Nursing Home, New Delhi. He was a healthy, chubby-cheeked baby who drew the admiration of our entire neighborhood. Like many new fathers, the birth of my firstborn made me reconsider my prospects. When Jan took Amby to Seattle to visit his grandparents, I was able to step back from the daily ins and outs of parenthood to really take a look at my hopes for my little family. I wanted my son's life to be easier than mine had been—for him to not have to worry about the cost of books or think about sharing a bicycle to get to and from school.

I enjoyed my job, but it had become clear that there wasn't as much opportunity for advancement as I'd hoped. Snowhite Engineers Pvt Ltd was a family business, and the owner's sons would inherit it. Maybe I would be able to get a few more promotions, a few more raises in salary, but there was a ceiling that, given my outsize aspirations, was much too low. On top of that, I was getting more and more frustrated with the bureaucracy in India through which seemingly every mundane interaction had to pass. Taxi and scooter drivers tinkered with their meters, and even just getting a cup of sugar or using the telephone required a bribe. That, in combination with the realization that my career would soon face a hurdle, had worn my patience thin. One day I got so frustrated that I called Jan and said, "I can't take this bureaucracy. And I don't see an opportunity here, unless we decide that we want to stay in India forever."

"OK," Jan said. I could hear Amby burbling in the background.

"You stay there, in Seattle," I said after a moment. "I'll come to you."

The day after my sister's marriage, in February of 1977, I was on a plane bound for Seattle. I had missed the first birthday of my firstborn, and I'd been in India for more than four years, eight months of which had been without Jan and Amby. During our separation, Jan had set up our new life. She was living with her father and stepmother, who took care of the baby while she was at her new job at Couden Insurance in West Seattle. She had even managed to save up a little money.

Back in the Pacific Northwest, I hit the ground running. Along with checking the newspapers, I used my privileges as an alumnus by going to the University of Washington's career center for help. Finally, after many interviews, I received three job offers: the first was from Chemithon Corp, a local manufacturer of detergent chemical plants, and the second was from Owens Corning, a ceramic and insulation company based on the East Coast.

The third, after a day of interviews and a tour of the plant in Richmond, California, was Chevron.

To make a very long story—the story of my entire career—short, I stayed at Chevron for the next thirty-two years, first in the role of research engineer at Chevron Research Co, then in various other capacities as I moved up the ladder. Despite management's initial reservations about promoting a man of my race, religion, and background, I went on to oversee the construction of the Richmond Lube Oil Project, in 1982, and the design of the Phosphate Fertilization Plant in Florida, in 1984. I would later become chief engineer of designs, then move on to an operating role and downstream projects coordinator in the Bay Area, in 1990. The introduction of the business case for diversity in the early 1990s affirmed what I had already been working to prove every day. I went on to become a group manager of the Projects and Engineering Technology division, then further into managerial and executive roles at Chevron and Caltex Australia Ltd, a public company with Chevron holding 50 percent of the shares. Often, each new role meant a new adventure for myself and my family, which had grown with the birth of Shamick (Shammi) Jeet Bindra in 1978. It also offered me many new opportunities for on-the-job learning, many lessons about how to acclimate to a new work environment, how to manage the tension that inevitably arises when a new boss comes around, and how to effectively lead from day one. These lessons I will now share with you.

Jan, Amby, and newborn Shammi waiting to go home from the hospital.

People have all kinds of reasons for moving around, and for leaving their families of origin and their hometowns. For some, it's a matter of life and death, a necessity due to violence or political oppression. For others, it's a matter of financial survival, of jobs vanishing or economic bubbles bursting. Still others have an intellectual or artistic passion—a drive that propels them away from what some might consider a more practical or safer avenue. Whatever the reason, the people who make these moves—refugees, immigrants, businesspeople, and entrepreneurs—are taking big risks in pursuit of better lives. They aren't waiting around for peace and prosperity to come to them, for a golden egg to drop into their laps. Instead, they seize opportunity when it arrives, and let go of the comfort of the known for the sake of possibility.

- How do you approach the unknown? Do you tend to view it with skepticism and fear? Excitement and optimism?
- How do the important people in your life approach adventure? Do you tend to be more adventurous or more cautious than those whom you are close with?
- How does your family unit (whatever that may be) deal with a big change? How do you get them on board with it?
- When weighing your options, do you tend to focus on the negative, on all the ways things could go wrong? Or do you focus on the positive, on the potential and where this adventure could lead?
- When presented with an opportunity for adventure, how do you come to a decision about whether or not to seize it?

GET TO KNOW YOUR TEAM

As you settle into a new role, meet with your direct reports one-on-one several times during the first few months. I suggest you have one or more of these meetings over lunch or dinner as a way to "break bread" in order to break down barriers and build trust. Learn the essentials about each person—the duties of their job, their hobbies, their sports team, and their families. In my experience, people love to talk about themselves, to share their lives and knowledge and expertise, so this is a good way to build a rapport. You will want to be somewhat open in talking about yourself, too. I always tried to be very candid in my personal introduction, to make sure to share with my new colleagues at least a couple of things about me and my life outside of work. I would tell them my hopes and admit to my fears and weaknesses. I wanted people to see me as a person, in the hopes that they would allow me to see them as whole people, too, and would feel more comfortable coming to me with their own hopes, fears, and weaknesses.

If you are in a position to do so, ask the audit department to review expense reports submitted by your direct reports for the preceding twenty-four months. You'd be surprised what you can learn from these audits—they give you a glimpse into the values and ethics of each individual.

Now, an absolutely critical task: **Remember the names of your employees**. This task requires practice and discipline, and though it may seem like a small thing, being called by name means a lot. I cannot overstate the importance of this in earning people's trust. While writing this book, I talked to many of my former colleagues about our time together at Chevron and in our friendships outside of work. Every single one mentioned my penchant for memorizing names; a few of them mentioned a dinner party in Wales in which they decided to put my skills to the test. Usually, in these occasions, I would raise a toast to all the attendees, mentioning each person by name. In this instance, there were about eleven members of the leadership team plus their spouses present, and when I left the dining room they all got up and moved around, so I wouldn't be able to use association to remember the husband's or wife's name. I remember walking back in to find their faces lit up. "I bet you can't remember all of our names now!" someone called out. I looked around the room, took a deep breath, and passed the test with flying colors. "You win, you win," a colleague said. "We'll never do it again."

Everyone has their own method, and I'd encourage you to develop your own. Here is what worked for me (if you don't have the resources of an assistant or human resources department, skip to #3):

1. Request the human resources department provide you with:

    - Name, date of birth, and spouse's name for all direct
      reports and their direct reports.
    - Start date of employment/service anniversaries for
      all employees in the organization.

2. Ask your assistant to:

    - Produce a pocket-size, laminated card with all the
      names of your direct reports, their email addresses
      or identification numbers, office and cell phone
      numbers, and, if possible, the names of their spouses
      and children.
    - Keep track of the birthdays of direct reports, and
      their direct reports, and, every month, organize
      birthday cards to send them. Be sure to personally
      sign each card before it goes out.
    - Send congratulatory emails to every employee on
      the fifth, tenth, fifteenth, twentieth, etc. service
      anniversary.

3. On your own, start to:

    - Make a mental decision to remember, or not remem-
      ber, a person's name when you meet them. Mental
      space is precious, so be clear about how you want to
      use it.
    - Engage each person whose name you intend to
      remember in a meaningful conversation during
      which you intentionally address them by their name
      at least a couple of times. For example, instead of
      simply asking, "What's your favorite restaurant in
      town?" I'll say, "*Carol*, what's your favorite restaurant
      in town?" This starts the process of registering the
      name in your mind.

- Jot down the names of team members you are meeting for the first time at a conference or small gathering in the order in which they are seated, and during the subsequent conversation refer to your notes and address each of them by name at least once. If you have the luxury of access to photographs, study these before and after meetings until you feel confident in your memory.

LISTEN TO EMPLOYEES

During the first sixty to ninety days, organize meetings with small groups of employees for the express purpose of listening and gathering information. Usually for these meetings, I'd plan an agenda that looked something like this:

1. **Introduce myself and state my priorities.** I believe that making an explicit statement of intent from the beginning helps to set the right tone and provide big-picture goals. From day one, I always made it crystal clear that my number one priority was safety. Be aware, however, that to say it aloud is to request to be held accountable—so be clear with yourself before you take that step. Ask yourself:

   - What are your top three priorities? Out of these, what is your number one priority?
   - How have you demonstrated your commitment to this priority in the past?
   - How do you plan to take actions that align with this priority going forward?

2. **Make clear that I am here to listen and learn.** I would also let them know that I might not agree with everything they told me, but that I would take their input into consideration as I made decisions going forward.

3. **Ask questions.**

   - What's working well?
   - What's broken?
   - What pisses you off about the organization?
   - If you were in my position, what is one thing you would change immediately?

At the end of every meeting, be sure to thank each participant for their valuable gift of feedback and tell them what you plan to do with it. For the areas you do agree with, be sure to follow through and implement those changes to earn credibility and trust.

LEARN THE BUSINESS

Engaging with employees in a more casual manner is a good way to get a general sense of employee satisfaction, but you will also need to get more specific information about the business. I spent the first thirty days learning the business or, in situations of geographic distance or great complexity, sixty to ninety days. The goal isn't to become an expert in this time but to know enough to ask the right questions. There is no such thing as a stupid question, but I'd recommend you use whatever business data is available to come up with ones that sound informed. Questions like:

- What are the key inputs and outputs? What are the key business drivers?
- Where is the value created? What is the cost structure?
- How is technology used?
- What is the competitive landscape?
- How is the organization performing, in both internal objectives and external benchmarks?
- Where are the soft spots—the areas of the organization that have a vulnerability or weakness?

- Where might there be opportunities for a step change in performance?

Along with meeting with direct reports one-on-one and in small groups, spend time with various teams—the leadership team, the finance team, and so on—in order to learn the business from different angles.

MAKE A 100-DAY PLAN

Once you have completed the process of gathering information from the entire employee base and have a level of comfort about the direction of the business, it is time to develop a 100-Day Plan. I recommend that you base this plan on consultant and corporate planner George T. Doran's SMART principles (Specific, Measurable, Achievable, Realistic, and Time-Based), and that it includes:

- Your commitments to your supervisor
- Specific actions that you personally plan to complete
- Specific actions you expect others to complete

I suggest you refrain from making radical moves, and instead focus on realigning the business as necessary. If the organization doesn't have a clear vision, mission, or objectives, then draw these up from scratch or work toward more robust articulation. Having a precisely outlined plan creates another level of accountability in the organization and allows you to model good behavior as you fulfill your tasks.

MAKE EVERY MEETING EFFECTIVE

I have sat through many meetings that didn't have clearly defined agendas—that came to feel like meaningless ambles through a myriad of useless information via disjointed conversations and presentations without purpose. These are the types of meetings that are satirized in movies and on TV, with their attendees watching the clock and nearly going crazy from boredom. This waste of time is something no business can afford. An effective manager always uses their time in a manner that delivers maximum impact. One of the key components of time management is making sure that meetings are designed to optimize the contribution of all the attendees. If you aren't sure whether you should schedule a meeting, consider whether a decision is necessary and ask yourself if the decision requires:

- Input and buy-in from several stakeholders
- Expert advice on a specific topic
- Timely resolution, for which seeking input via email or other means will delay decision-making beyond an acceptable timeframe

Once you establish that a meeting is necessary, it's time to get organized. Here are some of the key requisites for a successful meeting:

1. **Only invite employees when their participation is essential.** Each employee must have something to contribute to the decision-making process, as well as a stake in the final decision. Due to the global nature of business, it must be understood that one or more attendees may be joining the meeting late at night or very early in the morning, depending upon their time zones. If all attendees cannot join in person:

    - Pick a time for the meeting that minimizes discomfort for the majority of attendees. If this is an ongoing issue, try to spread the pain among the attendees by ensuring that the same people are not negatively impacted every time.
    - Use a video-conference program so that everyone can see the body language accompanying speech, which allows for better communication and prevents attendees from disengaging.

2. **Clearly designate roles**, including:

   - A chairman to preside over the meeting
   - A secretary to keep track of agreements and action items
   - A timekeeper who will monitor progress to ensure proper time management

3. **Define the decision-making process.** Often attendees arrive expecting a consensus process for decision-making while the leader only intended to seek input and then make the decision independently. This can lead to discord and significantly undermine the implementation of the decision. Six decision-making options are outlined below:

   A. The leader makes the decision, then tells or "sells" it.
   B. The leader proposes the decision, gets feedback from the team, and then the leader decides.
   C. The leader asks for the individuals or group to come up with and present options, then the leader decides.
   O. (For "optimal") The group (including the leader) decides by consensus.
   D. The leader or team identifies constraints and delegates decisions to an individual or subgroup. In this option, ground rules are clear for whether the group can:

      - Decide
      - Review a decision and figure out how to implement it
      - Decide, implement, and periodically inform the team about progress

   E. Individual or subgroups empowered by the leader take full responsibility for acting within the agreed upon context.

How can you select the right decision-making process? Consider time available for making the decision, the potential impact of the decision, the buy-in needed, the information and expertise of the team members, the professional developmental opportunity for team members, and leader flexibility. Use the following framework to select the decision-making process:

	A	B	C	O	D	E
Time Available	little	——————→		a lot	←——————	little
Potential Impact of Decision	low	——————→		very high	←———	low/ medium
Buy-in Needed	little	——————→		a lot	←———	little
Members' Information and Expertise	little	———————————————————→				a lot
Developmental Opportunity	low	———————————————————→				high
Leader Flexibility	nonnegotiable	———————————→				flexible

Option O is the most desirable process for most business decisions, for the simple reason that it is easier to implement a plan when every team member supports it. But achieving unanimous consensus is hardly ever possible. It is also not necessary for success if the entire team, including those who don't fully agree with the decision, is invested in implementing it. Therefore, it is important that all attendees understand what is meant by consensus and that rarely does this word indicate 100 percent agreement.

- Consensus is a decision made by a team that each member, including the leader, understands and is willing to actively support. Even if the decision was not their top personal choice, they do not see a fatal flaw.

- Consensus works best when there is a "fallback" decision-making process that the team is committed to using when necessary. For example, if a consensus can't be reached within the larger group, then decision-making authority will be given to a subgroup.

A mix of decision-making options may be used by a leader or group. For example:

- A leader might define the problem (tell) and request a team to develop possible solutions (input).
- A team may agree by consensus on a recommendation they will make to a leader or sponsor (input).
- A team may define the problem (consensus) and delegate authority for solving it to an individual.

There are three critical types of satisfaction in terms of this process:

- **Content satisfaction**: members are satisfied with the decision.
- **Procedural satisfaction**: members are satisfied with the process used to reach the decision.
- **Psychological satisfaction**: members are satisfied with how they were treated during the process.

In a perfect world, every attendee would experience all three; leaders must strive for psychological satisfaction at the very least. Here are steps that you can take to achieve this goal:

1. **Have a clear, crisp agenda, with clear objectives** that outline what you hope to accomplish by the end of the meeting. The agenda must identify the context, including unit or team vision and mission, goals and objectives, boundaries and limits, as well as roles and responsibilities, time allocated for each topic, the decision-making process, and outstanding issues from previous meetings.

Every meeting must have a clearly articulated agenda that is communicated to the attendees well in advance along with advance reading material. At the start of each meeting, review the outstanding issues before moving on to new objectives. A sample agenda is shown on the opposite page.

2. **Record every meeting and create a shared web-based folder** to share the minutes of prior meetings, updates on the issues addressed, the agenda for the upcoming meeting, and other material to be read prior, or the "pre-read." Make the pre-read available well in advance of the meeting to allow attendees time to prepare, and so that they can follow the discussion. Use flipcharts or create electronic buckets for:

  - **Agreements**
  - **Action Items**, those responsible for implementing them, current status, expected date of completion, and other notes
  - **"Parking Lot" Issues**, or those issues that are important, but do not have relevance to the objective(s) of the meeting—capture these issues in a separate folder and park them for others to address as appropriate

COMMUNICATE AND CELEBRATE

I believe that, in the absence of information, we humans have a tendency to start filling in the blanks, more often than not with negative assumptions. So it is very important to communicate as much as possible to eliminate potentially harmful misunderstandings. In the beginning, send regular monthly updates to all employees, using the 100-Day Plan as a basis for measuring progress. My communications, particularly those early ones, not only outlined what might change under my leadership but also what *would not* change. This is critical for eliminating the kinds of ambiguities that strike fear in the hearts of employees and can sometimes result in the building of animosity toward those

Sample Meeting Agenda

Meeting Date & Time: _____

Invitees: _____

_____

     Chairman: _____

     Secretary: _____

     Time Keeper: _____

Outstanding Issues: _____

_____

_____

_____

Objective(s): _____

_____

_____

_____

Topic: _____

Decision Required: Y / N

Decision-Making Process (A–E): _____

Time Allocated: _____

who have brought it about. If you don't know how something might change, be sure to note that, too—showing your own uncertainty will make you more relatable, and perhaps create a spark for new conversations. This comprehensive style of communication provides comfort to people who are worried that their world is being turned upside down and closes the loop on input received from employees during initial meetings. An aim of consistent communication is to **remain visible**, to make sure that **colleagues know your door is open**. Good leaders need to be accessible, and open to the insights, new ideas and, yes, the complaints of their employees. In order to encourage positive thinking and restate my priorities, I always ended my communications with the statement, "Please remain safe and continue to focus on the positives."

At the end of those one hundred days, continue this habit of monthly communication on business developments and use every opportunity to call out and reinforce good work. Such positive reinforcements can range from thank-you cards to ice cream socials to gifts commemorating a milestone achieved. If a big project has kept an employee away from home for long hours, send a card to their spouse once it's completed. These may be small in value, but they are meaningful as tokens of appreciation. As new targets are set and then hit, congratulate your team and celebrate their success. Success breeds success, and positive reinforcement helps to keep the momentum going. The same goes for you, too—for every new role you master, every milestone you hit, every promotion you earn, be sure to celebrate yourself, and thank those adventurous people who helped you to get there.

CHAPTER 3

FIGHT FOR TRUE INTEGRATION

Men had landed on the moon by the time I arrived in the United States in 1969, but the idea of someone with my ethnic background becoming president of a major company was considered pure lunacy. I joined Chevron in 1977, when the company was very conservative—not exactly on the cutting edge in promoting women and minorities into management positions. You didn't have to be a clairvoyant to see it— rarely did I encounter another person with brown skin in the halls of the corporate offices and most of the women I worked with were firmly in place behind their reception desks. I was certainly the only person with a long beard and a turban.

A couple of years after I started at Chevron, one of the company's vice presidents called me into his office.

"Jeet," he said, "you are an outstanding technical professional, no doubt. But because you look different, dress different, and speak with an accent, you'd be lucky to make it into middle management."

I have no idea why this gentleman felt the need in that moment to offer this little nugget of wisdom. I remember thinking, *Don't judge me by the color of my skin or my accent or the kind of food I eat or whether my name is Bindra, Wong, or Gonzales.* I had to work to keep my voice

level as I said, "Please judge me on my performance and what I bring
to the table." Then I left his office muttering a few well-chosen Hindi
expletives under my breath.

He probably thought I was terribly naïve. Maybe I was. But I chose
to take his comment not as an insult but as a challenge, and from that
day forward I was determined to prove him wrong.

I'm sorry to say that this was not an isolated incident. Other managers expressed reservations about my promotion to management
positions. Could I be effective in leading a group of white, male subordinates? Would the public at other Chevron operations—in San
Francisco or Pascagoula or Midland—accept me, or would they hesitate to work with me? Would promoting me help or hurt the business?

The Chevron of forty years ago is not the Chevron of today. When
I started working there, there were no awards for Best Workplaces for
Diversity, Best Places to Work for LGBT Equality, or Top 50 STEM
Workplaces for Native Americans. The word "diversity" as it is known
today was simply nonexistent in the social and cultural vocabulary.
After all, this was just thirteen years after Congress, under President
John F. Kennedy, enacted the Civil Rights Act of 1964, and the wheels
of justice are not known for their speed. Yet within the oil and gas
industry, Chevron actually led the charge in making change, starting
in the early 1990s. Like all trends, the thought trend of **diversity as a
competitive advantage** caught on one person at a time, until there
was critical mass and it started to feel more like an indisputable truth.

Women and minorities still have a big hill to climb, and though the
way to the top may seem daunting, it is not insurmountable. There is
a path to positions of power, made by the determined strides of those
who went before. Here is what you can do to get on it.

RESEARCH POTENTIAL EMPLOYERS' DIVERSITY POLICIES AND TRACK RECORD

Nowadays, there are awards for Best Workplaces for Diversity, and
there are online resources like Glassdoor and Best Places to Work
through which you can get a sense of a company's policies and track

record, as well as lists gathered annually by reputable publications like *Forbes*. Insight into companies' inner workings is more accessible than ever, and so not only are organizations working hard to show their dedication to equal opportunity and, increasingly, social justice, the workforce can see what kind of progress they're making, and whether a company would be a good place to work or not.

There's a catch-22 in this kind of transparency: people who value diversity may avoid working at companies in which diversity is lacking, and those same companies might have trouble recruiting people who hold diversity as a top priority. Had I, as a young South Asian man, looked at the status quo of Chevron and been deterred, this would be a different story. That is why I recommend you don't dismiss a company with a poor rating right off the bat and do your own research. You must:

- Talk to a human resources representative, a current employee, or a potential supervisor about their experience working at the company.
- Determine if there is room to grow, both within your own career and in terms of the company's evolution of its policy and practice.
- Find someone who holds the same values as you and will support you, both on a professional level and in working to build a diversity plan or some other effort to make a positive change within the company.
- Never let inequality stop you. Always try to convert adversity into an opportunity.

TAKE EVERY OPPORTUNITY TO SHATTER MYTHS ABOUT MINORITIES AND WOMEN

I met S. Shariq Yosufzai in 2001. I was on my way to Australia to take up the mantle as managing director and CEO of Caltex Australia Ltd, and he was heading back to California from a stint with Caltex in Singapore. In 2003, he became president of global marketing and I transitioned to become president of global manufacturing, the first time in Chevron history that two South Asians held jobs at that level at the same time. Basically, I did the making, he did the selling, and we got along wonderfully.

Many believe the stereotype that Indians and Indian Americans can only excel in the laboratory or as techies. Years ago, Shariq and I set out to show that South Asians could also be good leaders. We had our particular myths to shatter, just as those from other marginalized groups have their own. You've probably heard them all before. Minorities are lazy. They can't seem to finish a task on time, or communicate properly, or sell their ideas. Women are bad at math, or are too emotional, or are "distracted" by matters of motherhood and family. And, perhaps most insulting, women and people of color can't make decisions.

I believe these stereotypes have less hold as the years go by due to the laudable work of politicians, activists, and regular citizens who disprove them every day. Yet they still continue to exert some force, whether or not an individual or organization is aware of their influence. In my opinion, the two best ways to fight these myths are:

- Open discussion. Fortunately, this is in full swing in the media and in communities across the country.
- Simple exposure. Once you work alongside women and minorities, it becomes self-evident how ridiculous these myths are.

In time, I hope, these myths will be retired once and for all. Until then, you must:

- Contradict stereotypes by demonstrating that you can add value to the business through your dedication, creativity, and professionalism.
- Show that your background, however different it may be from those around you, is an asset, a way to disrupt outdated or status quo thinking.
- Work hard—and call out biases as you see them.

ADVOCATE FOR YOURSELF

Eventually I would be the first South Asian to get to the level of president within the company, and I'd like to say that this was because members of management were struck by a sudden epiphany. The reality was it took a lot of time and a ton of elbow grease. There were no epiphanies, and the tide of progress was slower than I might have liked. But I did not keep my head down and my mouth shut—I pushed back against prejudice and discriminatory practices and forged ahead. Like when members of the team responsible for selecting a candidate for a single-status twenty-eight days on / twenty-eight days off position in a remote area of Kazakhstan simply excluded the names of female candidates from the list. They assumed that a woman wouldn't want the job, that she'd have children to attend to and a household to run. I pointed out the sexism inherent in this assumption and insisted that we consider all candidates and, if a woman were selected, *she* should be the one to make the decision about whether to accept the position or not. I'm happy to say that one of the first women to take the assignment went on to become a senior executive at Chevron and, later, to serve on the board of directors of an international energy company.

I also made sure my good performance didn't go unnoticed. I used unjust treatment to fuel my passion, and to propel me to prove negative racial bias wrong.

Nirvana is the Hindu word for the place where we are free from life's trials and tribulations. We obviously haven't found nirvana yet when it comes to achieving true diversity in corporate America. The reluctance of white, male management, like the kind I experienced in the 1980s, has yet to disappear from the day-to-day realities of American business, and so you have to be ready to face prejudice head-on. You also need to go beyond your comfort zone. This means you will need to:

- Go out and meet people who are different from yourself while also cultivating a system of safety and support.
- Join professional organizations and attend conferences that are designed with you in mind as well as those that

will allow you to gain visibility, build new relationships,
and discover inroads.

The workforce is becoming more diverse, and more women and
minorities are coming into positions of power. So what does that mean
for other minorities and women who want to succeed? It means that
the brass ring is closer than ever, thanks to the hard work of those
who came before. But no matter how committed a company—or a
government, for that matter—is to diversity and inclusion, you can't
expect someone to hand it to you, and you can't depend on identity for
your career advancement. It is, and always will be, your responsibility
to advocate for yourself and to maintain your highest standards at all
times, to reach out and grab that brass ring and hold on. This may mean
that you have to stretch your thinking about yourself and what you are
capable of. A now-famous Hewlett Packard internal report claims that
men apply for jobs when they meet only 60 percent of the qualifications while women tend to apply only if they meet 100 percent. For
those who are looking for a new job or a promotion, ask yourself:

- Do you apply to jobs for which you *don't* fulfill all requirements? What percentage of requirements do you feel you
  have to meet in order to be comfortable applying?
- Do you have the aptitude and interest to learn what's
  necessary to be successful in this role? If you don't fulfill
  all requirements currently, do you believe that you would
  be capable of filling those gaps with additional training,
  education, or experience?

If the answers to these questions are yes, then go for it. The worst
thing that could happen is nothing. Still, if you don't get the job, find
ways to close gaps in your skill set—so that the next time you will be an
even stronger candidate—by volunteering on project teams or attending evening classes or seminars.

Together we work on fixing the system; individually, each person
is responsible for their perseverance and the standard of their work.
Don't let your contributions be ignored—seize every opportunity and

make the best use of your talents and the resources available to you. I would say that to anyone, whether you're male or female, black or white, a descendant of dukes or a descendent of dishwashers. But the fact of the matter is, if you are a women or person of color, then you are going to have to work harder than your white/male peers. And even if you *do* work harder there are no guarantees that you will end up at the same place, or in the same boardroom or country club or awards ceremony. I don't say that to discourage you; rather, just as I took that one manager's terrible comment about my unsuitability for promotion as a challenge rather than an insult, I hope that the current inequalities light a fire, that they motivate you to push yourself and your career to new heights.

***

I became group manager of projects and engineering technology in 1991, and despite doubts I proved effective in leading white, male subordinates. I continued to be promoted into management roles, as manager of strategic planning, Chevron Corporation, in 1994, and then as senior vice president of pipeline and transportation. In 1997, I became president of Chevron Pipeline Company in California.

Since the early 1990s, when Chevron's chairman and CEO introduced the idea of a business case for diversity to the board, the company has made incredible strides in creating an all-inclusive business organization through a concerted effort to hire and maintain a truly diverse workforce, one that accurately reflects the diverse customers served worldwide. These are the days of awards for Best Workplaces for Diversity, Best Places to Work for LGBT Equality, and Top 50 STEM Workplaces for Native Americans. Chevron has received those awards, as well as Asia Society Best Employer Awards, a Catalyst Award, and more. It has won a spot on the *Economist*'s Global Diversity List and the National Business Inclusion Consortium and National Gay and Lesbian Chamber of Commerce's Top 30 Companies for Diversity. The company has received recognition as a Top Supporter of Historically Black Colleges and Universities from *US Black Engineer and Information Technology Magazine*, recognition for its dedication to STEM diversity from Diversity in Action, and a score of 100 percent on the Corporate Equality Index from the Human Rights Campaign for the last thirteen years. In 2001, Chevron's board included one white woman and fifteen white men. At the end of 2017, out of a board of ten, five were white men, two were white women, two were African American women, and one was a Hispanic man.

Change can happen. There are no excuses for an inequitable workplace—it isn't easy, but diversity can be achieved.

I've spent my career figuring out best practices for solving a big problem, and it is through decades of experience that I have come to a conclusion, one you might find controversial: I don't believe in quotas. Now, let me tell you why: enforcing quotas opens up the possibility of compromising quality. You can look at it from the opposite side. When police have arrest quotas, there's a greater chance that highly problematic policies like "stop and frisk" will develop, because officers become more focused on hitting their numbers than on doing their job of protecting and serving. In a pinch, people tend to default to fear and "us versus them" thinking, rely on unexamined biases to make decisions, and succumb to power dynamics and hierarchal styles of relating. This was the case with stop and frisk—according to 2012 reports from the Center for Constitutional Rights and the Public Advocate's office, black people made up 53 percent of the stops, while representing only 25 percent of New York City's population.

You might be thinking, *That's all well and good. But if you don't mandate quotas, what* do *you do?* You **monitor efforts to build diversity and an ecosystem of inclusion**. The Chevron Way, a comprehensive document that explicitly states the company's vision and values, says, "We learn from and respect the cultures in which we operate. We have an inclusive work environment that values uniqueness and diversity of individual talents, experiences, and ideas." This is not lip service—the mission of diversity has been embraced companywide, and we've worked to define actionable directives and measurable standards. In every performance review, up and down the ladder, supervisors ask their employees, "What have you done to support and build diversity?" As the accolades show, our formal process of monitoring efforts has upheld the company's mission, yet without sacrificing the most important imperative of every business: to attract and retain talented people, regardless of race, color, sex, religion, or national origin.

As you climb the corporate ladder, start your own business, or find yourself in a position of power within some other realm, more responsibility for creating diversity will fall on your shoulders. So how can you convince others to implement policies and practices of inclusion, and what might these look like in operation on the ground?

ARGUE FOR DIVERSITY AS A COMPETITIVE ADVANTAGE

Because so much academic research and practical implementation has occurred in the last thirty years, these days it is much easier to demonstrate to even the most hard-nosed, profit-preoccupied leader why diversity makes business sense. Time and again, experts have shown that diversity is a competitive advantage. In 2018, global management consulting firm McKinsey & Company found that companies in the top quartile for gender diversity at the executive level were 21 percent more likely to experience above-average profitability compared to those in the bottom quartile, and companies in the top quartile of cultural and ethnic diversity were 33 percent more likely to outperform their less diverse competition. You don't recruit, hire, and promote in a bubble, after all, and along with having employees who can better represent your consumers—and therefore have a better idea of what consumer groups need and want—differences among team members provide essential balance both within the team and within the company as a whole. If you are building an eight-person team, you don't want to hire eight type As, or eight Ivy League alumni, or eight of your best friends from back in the neighborhood. A team with that makeup is much more likely to agree on everything, which might be satisfying in the moment, but I can guarantee it limits innovation. You want to bring in people who will, by their personality types, backgrounds, skill sets, and interests, cause a disruption and upset the status quo. Based on a survey of 1,700 companies across eight countries, the *Harvard Business Review* reported that the most diverse enterprises were also the most innovative. **Disrupt**

thinking through diversity: this is how you innovate. That is essential for keeping up in a fast-paced and ever-changing marketplace.

There are a growing number of books on disruption and diversity, such as Malcolm Gladwell's 2008 *Outliers*, Sheryl Sandberg's 2013 *Lean In*, and Mahzarin R. Banaji and Anthony G. Greenwald's 2013 *Blindspot* have topped and continue to top the bestseller lists. Publications like *Forbes*, the *Economist*, the *Wall Street Journal*, *Publishers Weekly*, the *Financial Times*, the *Harvard Business Review*, and consultancies and nonprofits like Deloitte, Catalyst, and McKinsey & Company offer evidence-based articles on how including women and minorities at all levels of a company benefits the bottom line. If your company doesn't have a diversity plan, you have a cornucopia of material one click away with which to make your case.

BROADEN YOUR SPECIFICATIONS

In the past, Chevron did most of its recruiting through select universities and the tried-and-true method of word of mouth and personal recommendation. The problem with these methods is that they rely on the established pipeline, created by a select group—white men— and which inherently favors members of that same group. Eventually my friend and colleague S. Shariq Yosufzai moved on to become vice president for global diversity, ombuds, and university affairs, and he worked to measure the success of diversity efforts at two levels: whom Chevron was recruiting into entry-level positions, and whom the company was identifying as executive and leadership material with potential for promotion.

To recruit a diverse workforce, you must build new pipelines and open doors to people who are different from yourself, your team, and those already inside the company. You must:

- Recruit at technical and diversity conferences.
- Search for talent in previously untapped locales.
- Do outreach at new educational institutions.
- Promote a message of welcome online.

- Dig deep within your organization to identify individuals who are willing to learn and grow.

To do my part in remedying the pipeline problem, I became involved both inside and outside the company as a corporate executive sponsor for Hispanic recruitment and as a founding chairman of the South Asian American Leaders of Tomorrow. I traveled around the country to speak at conferences hosted by groups like the National Society of Black Engineers, Los Ingenierios, the Society of Hispanic Professional Engineers, the Society of Women Engineers, and the American Society of Engineers of Indian Origin. Simply put, I wanted to make sure that people outside the company knew that the door was open to them. "Shoot for the moon," I'd tell the younger members of the audience, "and enjoy the ride."

To add dimension to the hiring and selection process, **build selection teams that are made up of diverse individuals**, both in terms of background and in terms of their positions within the company. An applicant's talent and personality appear differently from the top looking down than down looking up or looking out across a level plane. Human resources provides a valuable first contact, but the potential supervisor, a peer, a future subordinate, and someone from outside the department can bring in different and valuable perspectives on how the applicant looks from multiple angles.

Recruiting the most talented and the brightest is the first step. The second step is getting them to stick around, which requires a deep examination of promotion practices for employees once they have their foot in the door.

At the Chevron of twenty-five years ago, it was required that operating positions at the managerial level be filled by someone with extensive operating experience. A specification so narrow, however, automatically excludes a significant portion of talent. Upon close examination, we realized that an in-depth understanding of operations isn't truly essential to management, and a gap in knowledge can easily be supplemented through training and experience if the employee in question is interested and able. So, we asked ourselves, what if we prioritized technical and management experience, and looked for potential in terms

of ability and desire to learn about operating? We could surround a
new leader with team members who had deep operating and technical
backgrounds to help them fill in the gaps. That increased accessibil-
ity to the role considerably, and allowed us to bring on people with
more diverse backgrounds that had excellent management experience.
We even selected a career marketing professional to become a refinery
manager based on his leadership skills and willingness to learn.

We also must work to create points of entry further up the line.
When I took over as president of Chevron's global manufacturing, I
analyzed our system performance and learned that we suffered from
poor safety and reliability issues. We were wasting hundreds of millions of dollars due to the fact that some of our process plants had to
be shut down on a frequent basis. The solution to this problem eluded
us for a while, until finally we had to admit to ourselves that we didn't
know what we didn't know, and that we needed to bring in someone from the outside to give the problem a fresh look. The common
practice had been to promote from within, and trying a new method
meant taking a big risk. But we were stuck, plain and simple. After a
few months of searching, a headhunter delivered us Bruce Chinn, a
creative and intelligent man who happens to be an African American.
Right from the start I could see his potential. "Give him a chance," I
told my apprehensive colleagues. He didn't have all the exact on-paper
qualifications for the job, but he had an excellent track record and an
obvious capacity for mastering new skills and overcoming daunting
challenges. On top of that, he had the kind of personality and a penchant for collaboration that would make work with big egos go more
smoothly. We hired him as general manager of reliability for Chevron's
refining sector, he hired fifteen or so high-quality outsiders, and he
and his team were able to bring something new and different that was
needed to solve the problem.

When assessing a person for a new job or promotion, ask yourself:

- How do you judge quality?
- Do you look for someone to fit into a narrow mold,
  or are you open to different backgrounds, skill sets,
  personalities?

- What are the truly essential qualifications needed for the new role?
- What are skills and knowledge that can be acquired on the job?
- Does this applicant have a desire to learn and add to their skill set?

WELCOME CONSTRUCTIVE DISSENT

A critical element for promoting and maintaining diversity and an ecosystem of inclusion is to welcome new voices, new strategies, and, especially, constructive dissent. Each person must be held accountable for this: The hiring team ensures that there is a diversity of personalities, backgrounds, and experiences represented in the room, and that the team is made up of individuals with unique, complementary talents. The manager, and the company at large, is responsible for creating an atmosphere in which each team member feels comfortable voicing dissenting opinions, and for recognizing consistent agreement for the red flag that it is. To do so:

- Play devil's advocate if need be.
- Don't be afraid to table a discussion if the need for a decision isn't urgent.
- Tease out new ideas and constructive dissent from those with quieter personalities or who belong to a group with a history of being silenced.
- If you believe that an employee has an interesting idea that he or she didn't fully express in a meeting, then go afterward to their office. This is an important point: everyone gets nervous when called into the boss's office, and nervousness isn't conducive to open discussion or a brainstorming session. So visit the employee on their turf, where they are more likely to feel comfortable.

- Keep an open-door policy so that your team feels comfortable approaching you to lay out their viewpoint, even if it's one you don't automatically agree with.

TAKE A STAND AGAINST INJUSTICE, PREJUDICE, AND DISCRIMINATION

This bit of advice is, perhaps, the most difficult to follow, and one I would like to illustrate through a story about a situation in which I fell short.

In 2010, I applied for a board position at a big West Coast company. In lieu of a formal interview, I met with each board member individually, a common practice for selection. Each of the board members was an expert brought on to debate and decide on the big-picture issues of the day for the company, including companywide policies, goal planning, legal and financial challenges, and the vetting of top executives and other board members. To get a spot, you need to be at the top of your field, an expert in some aspect of business. In big companies, a board member's pay and hours are excellent, and it allows people to stay involved without being a part of the daily grind, making it highly desirable, particularly for those looking toward retirement. And, like most desirable high-level positions, white men have historically occupied most if not all available spots. The numbers are improving, though we have a long way to go. As of 2016, white women made up only 16.4 percent of Fortune 500 boards, with minority men coming in second at 10.6 percent and minority women in a distant third at 3.8 percent, according to a study by Deloitte and the Alliance for Board Diversity. During that same time period, only 19 percent of board candidates were minorities, and 16 percent of candidates were women.

Today I would be an outlier, and I certainly was back then. Still, I'd been a minority competing with mostly white men for advancement for the entirety of my career, and at this point such a trial didn't faze me. In fact, I hadn't thought once about my race when considering and negotiating board positions—I was more than qualified and had the exemplary track record to prove it, and no one in their right mind could argue with that. Frankly, after an over forty-year career in which

I climbed to the top of the corporate ladder in one of the major international energy companies in the world, a time in which I'd flown on private jets and drank vodka with Russian dignitaries, I'd grown accustomed to the comfort of my prestigious position, to people treating me with respect—this was something I felt I'd earned, though I do believe that **everyone deserves to be treated with respect**, whether they are the CEO or the mechanic. I had no doubt that, were I to walk into a conference room at the corporate offices or a Chevron refinery, I would find my colleagues behaving in a dignified manner, and acting with upmost professionalism toward their work and one another. I'd come to take it for granted.

This particular board had arranged a company limousine to pick me up at the hotel and take me to the home of the board member with whom I'd be meeting that day. At the gate to this gentleman's home, the driver punched in the code, and we slowly cruised up to the front of the house and came to a stop. I opened the door and got out. It was quiet, with not a soul in sight. I could hear the sound of a leaf blower in the distance, the unofficial background noise of California. After a moment, the front door opened and a white man whom I guessed to be around my age stepped out. On the front stoop he froze, cocked his head to the side, and scowled. He didn't say anything.

"Hello," I said, stepping forward and offering my hand. He still didn't move. "Um, I'm the prospective board member. Jeet Bindra."

"Ah," he said, and then shook my hand.

It wasn't until a couple of months later, after I'd been accepted to the board, that I found out some unfortunate information about that strange interaction. All of us board members were at the chairman's house, having a nice dinner of medium-rare steak and good red wine. The gentleman who'd acted so strangely—I'll call him "Jonathan"—was sitting across from me. After a glass and a half of cabernet sauvignon, I said, "Jonathan, do you remember when I first met you at your house? You gave me a really strange look."

"Oh yeah," he said, wiping his mouth with a cloth napkin. "I took one look at you and thought I was about to be robbed."

For me, time seemed to stop for a second. I thought back to that moment at Jonathan's house—I had just gotten out of the *company*

limousine in this man's gated driveway, for which you needed a security code, for Pete's sake. There was no reason, absolutely *no reason*,
why Jonathan would have thought he was being robbed. It was a crazy
assertion, really, and a harsh reminder that, for a few people, my
accomplishments and my expertise wouldn't matter, that some people
would take one look at me and jump to the most ridiculous and racist
conclusions. It had been so long since I'd experienced treatment of this
kind that I'd almost forgotten what it felt like. Perhaps I'd even come
to assume that I'd somehow escaped it or graduated from it, and that
I would never again meet someone who would assess me in such a
profoundly disrespectful way. I thought my nice clothes, my expensive
haircut, my impressive resume, and my time spent with top officials
and high-level executives all across the globe had inoculated me.

Out of the two of us, Jonathan should have been the one to feel that
sting of humiliation. But in that moment, I was surprised, and embarrassed, and completely caught off guard. Even though I had worked
so hard to fight against the stigmas of racism, I didn't know what to
do. I glanced around the table at my fellow board members, trying to
catch their eyes. As far as diversity was concerned, this board was well
above average. At the time of this incident, along with six white men,
it included me, one African American man, one Hispanic woman, one
Hispanic man, and one Asian American woman who, I would guess,
were just as tired as I was of trying to manage the bad behavior of
others—any marginalized person will tell you how exhausting contin-
uously pushing back against injustice can be. The discomfort in the
room was thick enough to cut with a steak knife. No one said anything;
everyone kept on eating, sipping their wine, and avoiding my gaze.

I wish I had handled things differently. If I could go back in time, I
would have called it out in the moment, instead of waiting until resentment had accumulated to the point of no return. When I edit the memory, instead of getting back to the meal, I put down my fork and, in a
forceful voice, say, "That is unacceptable." Then I walk out.

In reality, after dinner, one of my fellow board members took me
aside. "That's just Jonathan, you know," he said. "You should ignore him."

If that was the way Jonathan behaved toward his peers, it wasn't
hard to imagine how he treated his subordinates, that he overlooked

performance and judged on the basis of race and gender—he'd already demonstrated as much. So, for the sake of not just myself but for all the people he came in contact with on a regular basis, I should have taken action. But I didn't want to bring shame on a company because of one bad apple, I told myself, and so I bit my tongue.

This phenomenon occurs all too often: a person in a position of power behaves inappropriately, and instead of having to face the repercussions of his actions, those he's mistreated are obliged to stay quiet and carry on. More often than not, it's because it is their job on the line, not his. How can you effectively deal with this?

- **Speak up during or immediately after the incident,** whether you are the one experiencing discrimination or you are a witness to someone else's experience of discrimination. (This is particularly important when you reach a position of power.) Doing so can be very uncomfortable, but it is essential that you go on the record. I believe that more often than not the person or people involved aren't aware of their problematic behavior and, when it is brought to their attention, they will voluntarily and sincerely make efforts to change it.

- **Insist on remedial action.** If no efforts to improve are made, or you feel too uncomfortable to speak directly to the perpetrator, then approach his or her supervisor or a human resources representative. The person should be subjected to progressive discipline, which is different in every company. For example, the perpetrator should get a warning, followed by mandatory attendance at diversity training, followed by unpaid time off. If they have a gross infraction or, after all those measures, they continue to diverge from the company code of conduct, they should be terminated.

- **Seek support outside the company.** If approaching a supervisor doesn't work, look elsewhere. This could include industry gatekeepers, women's or minorities' associations to which you belong, or even the media.

Sometimes companies need industry or public disap-
proval as motivation for implementing new policies and
better oversight.

- **In any case, work to ensure companywide policies
  that protect women and minorities are in place and
  being followed.** This is absolutely, without a doubt, the
  most important piece in the solution to racial and gender
  inequality.

I admit, with deep regret, that I failed to push the issue of discrimination on this big West Coast company's board. Over the seven
years of my tenure, Jonathan made many comments that diminished
others. He looked down on the company's employees, never bothering
to understand the work of those he considered his inferiors, and he
certainly didn't have a filter when it came to making comments—or,
as he seemed to think of them, "jokes"—about his professional peers.
I didn't always remain silent, however; in fact, at one point, I told the
chairman just what I thought. After another incident in which everyone looked the other way while Jonathan was "just being Jonathan," I
couldn't hold back.

"Jonathan is the most ignorant, racist person I've ever dealt with," I
said. "An MBA degree doesn't mean anything." Unfortunately, instead
of acknowledging my assessment, the chairmen sat there, stone-faced.
I should have seen this as a signifier—a clue to the board's true values.
Even though corporate America may have made major strides in identifying, recruiting, nurturing, and promoting women and minorities
into the middle and senior levels, it has failed to eradicate issues of
discrimination in its boardrooms. If there were only a single individual
on the board who had discriminatory tendencies, he or she wouldn't
have lasted very long, so it was more than likely that Jonathan's views
were supported by one or more members. There are still people who
are sympathetic to this kind of view, and we need to work to achieve
the day when boards are free from any decisions based on race, color,
creed, or other such considerations.

Years later, that same chairman retired, and it was up to us on the
board to find his replacement. And so we sat down and put together

a list of the criteria for potential candidates. Once that was finalized, three board members formed a selection team, which, unbeknownst to the rest of us, modified the criteria to disqualify candidates who hailed from parts of the world outside California. To be considered, a candidate would have to be a full-time resident of the state of California. The rationale they gave us was that it was a Californian company and so the chairman needed to be available to meet with the executives, as well as regulators and politicians. This was not a reasonable stipulation—the board met only a few times a year, and those of us who were not full-time residents could easily make arrangements to attend meetings in California whenever necessary. I believe that this was part of an intentional effort to rule out most women and minorities from square one.

When all this came to light, I told them, "You didn't like the answer you got so, without the board's consent, you changed the criteria to get what you want." A white man was hired for the position of chairman that same year.

I resigned from the board soon thereafter.

FIND THE DIAMONDS IN THE ROUGH

I like to compare a top-notch employee or executive to a precious jewel. The value of a diamond varies greatly, just as employees do. Some are brilliant, some are paste. A diamond's value is determined based on the four Cs: color, carat, clarity, and cut.

Color doesn't play as great a part in determining value as you might think. The Hope Diamond is blue, while the Portuguese Diamond is yellow—both are considered priceless. Yet when it comes to determining human value, color seems to play an outsize role. Somehow, we expect executives to be colorblind as they consider an employee for advancement, but of course the only way to be truly colorblind is to be truly *blind*. I believe that, instead of attempting this impossibility, executives need to recognize the rainbow of colors among their employees, understand those variations, and help them achieve the brilliance of which they are capable.

Carat, in this metaphor, refers to inherent abilities, our intelligence and capacity to learn and grow. There are just as many human carats among minorities as there are among the majority—the trick is to find those diamonds in the rough, to identify those carats early on, then nurture them toward their full potential. This is the polishing of the gem that makes a diamond's **clarity and cut** superior, just as mentoring and providing opportunities bring out an individual's performance excellence. Selecting high-carat individuals for these development opportunities is essential for improving their clarity and cut.

I hope that, someday, the word "diversity" won't refer to skin color, religion, gender, race, or any of the other superficial markers of difference. For now, we use these faulty identifiers as a kind of shorthand for new thoughts and ideas, via the people whom we judge based on accent or headdress. It is my belief that eventually we will recognize how ridiculous these categorizations are and move on to the phase where we truly judge one another by the contents of our character and intellect, our capacity for hard work, and our desire to learn. We will seek out difference and celebrate it, welcome it into classrooms and boardrooms, and understand it for the boon that it is.

CHAPTER 4

BELIEVE YOU HAVE A CHOICE

A few years after one of Chevron's vice presidents took it upon himself to share his doubts about my fitness for management, I was busy overseeing the design of the Richmond Lube Oil Project. Despite my attire and accent, my talents had been recognized and were propelling me up the corporate ladder. It wasn't until after a couple of quick promotions that, all of a sudden, I hit a barrier—one that prevented me from climbing into upper management.

One sunny afternoon, my then-current boss called me into his office. Like all men at his level—at the time, it was indeed *only* men— he was dressed smartly, wearing a three-piece, pinstriped suit and shiny, wing-tipped shoes. "You are doing extremely well, and you have a bright future ahead," he said. "Now that the design is nearing completion, we want you to manage the construction of the process plants for the Richmond Lube Oil Project."

I tried to contain my excitement. This would be a huge step up. I started to say something, but he held up his hand to stop me. "However," he continued, "we have an important safety rule that requires each and every employee working within the refinery to be smooth-shaven and with short hair. This is an OSHA requirement, and it's nonnegotiable.

If there were a chemical release and you put on a face mask, your hair would get in the way, and the mask wouldn't be able to seal. You'd not just be putting your own life in jeopardy, you'd be making yourself unavailable to help others should there be an emergency."

I sat back in the chair and stared at the ceiling. My boss went on, "I'm not saying that you won't be able to move up if you don't take this job. But if you decide not to cut your hair—which is, after all, your choice—then you will always be limited to the office jobs."

I nodded, then thanked him and stood up.

"I will think about it," I said.

I went home to talk it over with my wife, and ruminate and pace the floor of our bedroom. To my thinking, I had two very basic choices: I could either shave my beard and cut my hair and have access to a wider range of opportunities, or I could keep my hair and beard and possibly stall my career. Obviously, this was not a mere personal style choice—this was a choice about identity, about what I really wanted and what I was willing to give up to get it. How far would I go to fit in? How far would I go to succeed?

Hair is of special importance in the Sikh religion. To greatly simplify a complex history, Sikhism is an offshoot of Hinduism that is only a few centuries old, consolidated as a resistance movement in response to Mughal rule during the middle of the second millennium. My ancestors were warriors, and as such they developed a list of five articles of adornment to both aid in guerrilla warfare and serve as reminders of faith—what are now known as the Five Ks. These are:

1. Kesh: uncut hair
2. Kara: a steel bracelet
3. Kangha: a small comb
4. Kaccha: a cotton undergarment
5. Kirpan: a steel sword

We Sikhs still consider ourselves to be freedom fighters, but over time the types of objects and their symbolism have evolved. It is no longer feasible to walk around a city center or attend a board meeting wearing a full-size sword, for example, and the steel bracelet is rarely used as an arm guard during battle, as it was in centuries past. Yet a large number of us continue to forego cutting our hair and, like so many religious people throughout the world, we hold to the tradition of keeping our hair covered.

I had maintained this symbol of my faith for the nearly fifteen years I'd been in the United States. I had never left the house without my turban—called a "*dastaar*"—and Jan, my sons, and close family members were the only Americans who'd ever seen me without it. Many times, people had asked me about it, in both friendly and not-so-friendly terms, and many times supervisors and coworkers hinted at its removal, in subtle and not-so-subtle ways, but still I managed to hold on.

A couple of long and tense days after that conversation with my boss, I went to Leon's Barbershop, one of those homey one-man operations, located in El Cerrito. After I told him the scope of the project, he said, "Come back on Friday at closing."

As evening fell at the end of that week, I returned to the barbershop. Once inside, Leon shut the door and locked it behind him. We were alone. "Go ahead," he said, motioning to my turban. I reached up, carefully removed it and put it aside, then unwound my topknot and let my hair fall to its full length. In all my thirty-five years, it had never seen a pair of scissors; it reached down past my waist. Leon stared at me for several seconds, then held up a finger. "Hold on," he said. He returned from the back of the shop a minute later carrying a bottle of scotch and two glasses.

"I don't drink hard liquor," I told him.

"That's fine," he said, putting the glasses down on the counter in front of the mirror and pouring a couple fingers' worth of the scotch into one of them. "But I'm going to need one before I start on this project."

One-and-a-half hours later, I walked out of the shop without my turban. My head felt lighter, my neck longer, and suddenly I was acutely aware of seemingly every hair follicle as the breeze picked up.

"Is that you, Daddy?" a seven-year-old Amby said when I walked through the door.

I cannot overstate how unsettling this whole endeavor was to me—it continues to be one of my life's most traumatic experiences. I took the following week off, during which I spent more time in front of the mirror than I had in my whole life. Each first glimpse was a shock, a moment of disorientation and unrecognition. *Who is that?* I'd think before remembering that the person in the mirror was, in fact, me.

By the next Monday I was feeling better, or at least adjusted enough to find some fun in the situation. That morning, I approached the reception desk at my office. "I'd like to speak to Mr. Bindra," I said.

"He's not here yet, sir," the receptionist replied. I smiled and didn't say anything. She looked at me, a confused expression on her face. After a moment, her eyes lit up. "Mr. Bindra!" she said.

This was the toughest decision of my career. I believe, however, that the obvious practicality of it made it somewhat easier. It was an A plus B equals C equation: my hair was a safety hazard, and if I cut it, I would be promoted. So, after careful consideration, I elected to cut my hair and, by default, adopt a more corporate look. I didn't consider this choice to be "selling out." It didn't change who I was, who I *am*. Simply put, I was willing to alter my outward appearance to comply with safety requirements and to improve my chances for continued career progression. And it worked—the senior executives noticed and acknowledged the sacrifice, and soon I was working in the refinery on the construction of the Richmond Lube Oil Project.

Decisions involving identity and integration aren't always so clear-cut, with such a straight arrow from cause to effect. There are no branches of a law firm or tech company in which hair would be a safety hazard, and I'll never know what sort of choices I would have made had I been working in either of those environments. Perhaps I wouldn't have cut my hair. Perhaps I would have. But the point I am trying to make is that you have choices, possibly ones for which you will never know the exact impact, but choices nonetheless. And the way you present yourself is not necessarily a definitive picture of who you are. So how can you make these tough decisions about yourself and your presentation as you move through the world?

DEFINE SUCCESS

Toward the end of my career at Chevron, I traveled around giving keynote remarks at various organizations for engineers from different minority groups. At one in which the audience members were of Indian origin, I noted the impression of success that they gave, with their nice clothing and new cars parked in neat rows outside. I then asked, "If Mahatma Gandhi were here, would he think we had achieved the pinnacle of success?

"He might suggest that we're not doing enough to contribute to the 'success' of our Motherland, for instance. Or that we're not doing enough to help the downtrodden in India break the cycle of poverty. Or that we're not doing enough for future generations here in our new adopted home, the good ole US of A. Are we doing enough, he might ask, to ensure fair and equal treatment for all Americans? Are we doing enough to hasten the day when this nation will judge all of its citizens 'not,' as Martin Luther King, Jr. said, 'by the color of their skin, but by the content of their character'?"

To me, these historical figures were paragons of moral judgment, and I made the assumption, based on our shared cultural background, that others in the audience held them in the same light. I know some Christians who, in the same vein, ask themselves, "What would Jesus do?" when considering the next step in their paths. Some people look up to activists and religious leaders; others try to emulate an entrepreneur, public speaker, teacher, or personal mentor. Many view more than one person as an example of success. Remember, you can have more than one "mandir," or place of worship; you don't have to put all your efforts into just one goal, and different modes of operation are appropriate for different venues. Being a successful parent might look different than being a successful businessperson, though they will likely share common values—integrity, patience, reliability, responsiveness—and of course you can be both. For all your various roles, identify people who are successful in ways that resonate with you, then study their examples as you shape your own daily choices and long-term goals.

Not everyone aspires to upper management or, even if they do, believes it is worth an action as extreme as the one that I took to get there. Some people want money or accolades, to make a great discovery, lead a life of service, be a loving caregiver, follow a creative muse or a spiritual path. Or all of the above. No one can define success for you; it is up to you to define it for yourself. Ask yourself:

- What is your definition of success?
- Who do you know, personally or as a public figure, who exemplifies your definition of success?

WEIGH YOUR OPTIONS

As I touched on in chapter 1, once you establish what success means to you, you will need to figure out a battle plan for getting there by identifying the obstacles in your path. My fight came in the form of adapting my style of presentation, and actively seeking out feedback on areas of weakness and what I'd have to do to stay competitive. In 1977, five years before my transformation at Leon's barbershop, my supervisor, Dr. Walt Bollen, became my mentor and champion. He did not accept others' doubts about my potential—in fact, many years later, at a dinner party celebrating his mentorship, he would confess that he had maneuvered to send me in his stead on an important trip to Japan, which put me in the sightline of a senior manager from the Corporate Engineering Department and opened the door for an appointment for me to work on the Richmond Lube Project. When I told him about my ambitions, he encouraged me to register for night classes in the Executive MBA program at St. Mary's College of California, located outside of San Francisco. For two years I made the fifteen-mile drive up to the town of Moraga two or three times a week. At the same time, Dr. Rich Vose, one of the chief project managers, took me under his wing. He said, "Jeet, there are three things you really need to improve. First, you speak too fast. You need to slow down. Second, you look very serious, which can be intimidating. Put a smile on your face. Third, your accent. People have a hard time understanding what you are saying."

I knew he was right, and was grateful for his help. (Back then, the act of telling a woman or person of color to smile wasn't as politically loaded as it is today. And, of course, I had *solicited* advice.) Whenever I had to give a presentation, he'd draw a big smiley face with the words "slow down" at the top of my notes. I would take a calming breath and cut my pace by half, remembering to pause and shift my expression into a friendlier pose. Dealing with the accent was more difficult, and when I brought this up with Walt, he said, "I'll talk to HR and see if they can help you." They located an organization within driving distance of my work, and so, while near San Francisco for graduate school, I went in for two hours a week to practice my pronunciation, smooth out my Indian accent, and translate the Queen's English I'd learned in India into an American dialect.

I graduated with honors from St. Mary's College's MBA night program in 1979 and, armed with two master's degrees—chemical engineering and business—and more clearly enunciated English, I requested a transfer to Chevron's Project Management group. Lo and behold, my request was granted.

When making your own battle plan, introspection is essential, as is the outside assessment of a trusted friend or mentor. You will have to put aside moral judgements around whatever impediments you discover—whether it's your own deficit or a broader culture of exclusivity that is to blame—and take a neutral stance in weighing your choices. There is always something new to learn, after all, and expanding your self-knowledge and knowledge of the world in which you live can only make your choices more informed. Ask yourself:

- What are some blocks to your success that you or a trusted mentor have identified?
- What can you do to remove those blocks?
- What about you is negotiable? What about you is nonnegotiable?
- Would the sacrifice be worth it? What would you lose by making changes in the way you present yourself? What would you gain?

- How could you make changes in your presentation without feeling like you are "selling out" or compromising your values?

BE PROUD OF YOUR HERITAGE

There are some who might say that I had to give up too much of myself to get where I am today. Perhaps they think I'm a *"nakli"*—a fake or phony. Some might call me a coconut—brown on the outside, white on the inside. They have it reversed. On the outside, I'm a former president of Chevron, a successful businessman in white corporate America. On the inside, I am who I've always been—an Indian boy sitting on a jute mat learning to write, a new immigrant with eight dollars and the clothes on his back, a husband and proud father of two, a devout Sikh who takes time every day to pray. I didn't have to denounce my heritage to get where I am. I just look a little different.

I happen to believe that you can join the mainstream without losing your cultural identity, your individuality, or your ties to your family. When I cut my hair, in 1982, long natural locks, mullets, and Jheri curls were all the rage. Given that, I would guess that I wasn't the only man during that post-1970s era to sacrifice long hair for his career, nor the only person to have to wrestle with issues of identity and employment. Surely other men—even white men—had to make hard choices about their appearance and presentation. Though their hairstyles might not have held as much cultural significance as one tied to religious faith, to each individual it probably meant something personal and even profound. Perhaps they, too, came to the conclusion that sporting short hair and a suit didn't change their values or history—they could still be hippies or rockers or surfers on the inside.

The clothing you wear, the style of your hair, or the pace of your speech are only a small and superficial part of you. Whatever you choose to do to survive and to thrive, remember that it is your own unique history that made you who you are and, at the end of the day, that uniqueness is an asset you bring to whatever table you sit at.

***

In April of 1980, two years before I cut my hair, Jane Doty MacKenzie was finishing up her chemical engineering degree at the University of Michigan. She had arrived at Chevron for a site visit, a round of interviews, and lunch with a potential manager, just as I had three years before. She was young and bright, among the top of her class, a four-year varsity volleyball team member, with professional internship experience at General Motors, and, obviously, an excellent track record. Unfortunately, she ran into a problem right off the bat. The first manager she interviewed with sat down and told her without blinking an eye, "Women don't make good engineers."

I'm glad to say that she went to Human Resources and said, "If I'm not going to be treated as an equal contributor, then I'm not interested." The hiring representative did her best to assure Jane that that manager's statement did not reflect the company's beliefs. Still, at our prearranged lunch, Jane told me what had happened and said, "I would like to cancel the rest of the interviews scheduled for this afternoon. I don't need to waste my time."

"Please," I said, hoping to show her that not everyone at the company was sexist, and that there were opportunities for those who happened to not be white men, "at least give me a chance. You're here already, so why don't you come and meet my team instead?"

She agreed—later she told me that my turban signaled to her that there might be room at Chevron for those who didn't fit the traditional mold.

A month later, Jane graduated and took off on a backpacking trip around Europe. Chevron had sent her a job offer, but she had not yet responded. Someone as talented as Jane would have had plenty of offers. So, since I had not heard back from her, I called her and ended up talking to her mother. Not once, but two or three times—I was determined to clean up the mess that manager had made. When Jane got back, her mother told her, "There's been a couple calls from a guy named Jeet Bindra. I think you should work for him."

She started working for me that August as a chemical engineer, and though I moved on to a new role three months later, I did my best to give her the stretch projects she deserved. She proved again and again her aptitude, diligence, adaptability, and ability to think on her feet. Eventually she went back to school to get an MBA from Berkeley's evening program, then on to strategic planning, large-scale change leadership, and workforce and leadership development. After thirty-five years at Chevron, Jane retired as general manager for global workforce development. I'm glad to report that, according to her, that first interview motivated her to prove she could be a high contributor.

I did not do anything special for Jane; I did not do her any favors because she was a woman. I was interested in her because she was an exceptional candidate. With her permission, I am using her as an example to show that there will be a few bad apples who eliminate you from the running based on attributes you *cannot* change. I could change the length of my hair, the heaviness of my accent, and my level of education; I could not change the fact of my skin color. Jane could not change her gender. This is where personal choice confronts the need for systemic or cultural change, where we as a society must confront our biases and update our policies to be more inclusive. It is also a rallying cry, a call for all of us who are marginalized to come together and take collective action, and to gather as a unified force to build bridges and tear down walls. And it is an opportunity to prove the prejudiced who harm us through words and actions wrong. Here is how we can make choices that will benefit all of us.

BUILD BRIDGES WITH OTHER MARGINALIZED GROUPS

Some of you may recall how scary it was to be a minority after 9/11. Every day there was another news story about a hate crime in the wake of this tragedy. Within five days, more than six hundred hate crimes had been reported, most of which were aimed at people of Middle Eastern and South Asian heritage, though people of other races and ethnicities were caught in the sudden violence as well. Mosques were vandalized and Muslims were threatened and denied their right to practice their religion. A group of "dot busters" harassed South Asian American women for the bindis on their foreheads. A Sikh gas-station owner was shot to death in Mesa, Arizona, on September 15, because the perpetrators thought he was in league with bin Laden. A white man killed a Japanese American grocery-store owner in the suburbs of Chicago because he "looked foreign." Obviously, all of these people were innocent, targeted because of their looks, the color of their skin, and the style of their dress.

In my experience, far too many of my fellow South Asians make a distinction between the ethnic groups to which we belong. We may know the cultural differences between a Sri Lankan and a Nepalese, but most other Americans can't or don't care to tell the difference between us, or even between brown people in general. I'd go so far as to say that some people tend to blend us all together as "foreigners," whether we were born and raised on American soil or not. I, for one, have been called any number of things—an Arab, an Iranian, a Mexican, even an Italian. All this is to say that we, the marginalized, are in this together, whether we like it or not. If people enthralled by hate lump us all into one broad category, then we might as well join together for our shared best interests. There's an old saying: "The whole is more than the sum of its parts." Some credit the Greek philosopher Aristotle with this observation, one that continues to be relevant more than two thousand years after it was made. According to the 2017 census, there are approximately 4.4 million Asian Indians in this country—nearly equal to the entire population of the state of Kentucky. If you added that to the total number of African Americans and Latino Americans, minorities currently make up more than one-third of the total population. This amounts to over 117 million non-white Americans out of approximately 325 million total. If you factor in women as a distinct group, you could consider more than 50 percent of Americans as marginalized to some degree. As individuals, our powers can only reach so far. But imagine what we could accomplish if we minorities and women put our differences aside.

At the end of 1947, Jawaharlal Nehru said, "We must constantly remind ourselves that whatever our religion or creed, we are all one people." He was talking to the new nation of India, but his words apply to everyone, particularly as technology and mass migration blur the lines between us across the globe. In a multicultural country like the United States, nothing much can be gained by retreating behind the self-imposed walls of your own ethnicity by creating little Indias or Polands or Egypts in this country. There is nothing wrong with social-izing with friends of the same ethnic background, to create a safe haven of familiarity within the larger sphere of White Christian America. But we must **take advantage of the rich diversity this country has to offer**. We must build bridges with other minority groups, build con-sensus on issues critical to our communities. The best way to do this is on the ground—to share our cultures, our values, and our heritages by welcoming others to participate in our lives. Invite your American-born relatives to a home-cooked Indian dinner, non-Jewish friends to your Passover seder, heterosexual couples to your same-sex wedding, and Muslim neighbors to your Chinese New Year's dragon dance. And, as always, be open and curious about cultures different than your own.

Of course, there is no solution that will fit us all. But, to para-phrase President John F. Kennedy, "We must explore what problems unite us instead of belaboring those problems which divide us." The United States is a great country, perhaps the greatest in the world when it comes to granting its citizens personal liberties and opportunities to achieve what their individual energies and skills will allow. But it's not a perfect country by any measure, and we have a long way to go in civil rights and other important issues. So get out there and make your voice heard by:

- Actively participating in the democratic process at the local, state, and national levels. Vote!
- Understanding the voting records of our elected offi-cials and publicizing them so your community can make informed decisions about candidates running for office.
- Supporting causes you cherish by contributing financially to organizations that support your ideals, not just your temple, gurudwaras, church, or mosque.
- Volunteering your services and challenging young people to do the same.
- Asking yourself: Am I doing enough to make this country a better place to live?

LET YOUR PERFORMANCE SPEAK FOR ITSELF

Some of my fellow South Asians object to the label of the "model minority." I choose to embrace it. If I'm to be stereotyped, I'd rather it be as diligent, intelligent, ethical, and successful. I always worked hard to prove that particular stereotype right, but I never relied on it to clear the way for me. As I mentioned in chapter 3, I do not believe in quotas and, at the risk of being controversial, I will admit that I do not support affirmative action. White men should not get ahead based on race and gender, and women and minorities shouldn't expect to either. At the same time, you might as well expect to have to **work harder than your white, male counterparts**. This may sound unfair, and that's because it is. But would you rather get the corner office because you are a minority or woman, or because you earned it? Don't ever give anybody the chance to question your integrity, to say that you didn't give 100 percent to your job. I will let you in on a secret: if you want to rise to the top, not only will you have to work harder than your white, male counterparts, you will have to work harder than *everyone*.

I believe that high performance is the best weapon, not just individually, but as a means for creating inclusivity so that our children and grandchildren won't have to work so hard to blend in. Change is slow, but it happens. In 2009, Indian American emergency-room doctor Kamaljeet Singh Kalsi was allowed to serve in the US army while wearing a beard and turban. "We can be Sikhs and soldiers at the same time," he said in an interview with the *New York Times*. Darsh Preet Singh was the first turbaned basketball player in the NCAA, in 2015. In 2017, the United States got its first female Sikh mayor in Preet Didbal, and in 2018, Gurbir Grewal, in his full beard and turban, was confirmed as New Jersey's attorney general.

My hope is that, as our successes become more conspicuous than our *dastaars* or hijabs, headdress will be viewed with the same calm as any other article of clothing, and that the same acceptance will be applied elsewhere, so that people won't have to make such difficult choices around identity and presentation. Someday, people won't have to worry about speaking in a low voice to be taken seriously, or being dismissed because of an accent or body type. Perhaps someday merit will truly be the only thing that matters.

CHAPTER 5

ENGAGE HEARTS AND MINDS

Rarely is a phone call first thing in the morning good news. So when the phone number of Chevron Pipeline Company's central region district manager, Jerry, showed up on my caller ID at 6:30 a.m. on a winter's day in 1999, I knew chances were high that this wasn't going to be a fun conversation. I picked up the phone. "Jerry?" I said tentatively.

"Jeet," he said by way of greeting. "There's been an accident at our pumping station near Fort Worth. An explosion. A welder has been badly burned."

"Is he OK?" I asked. Then, after Jerry didn't say anything, I amended the question. "Will he survive?"

"We hope so," he answered, "but we don't know."

I quickly got dressed and hopped in the car for the four-hour drive to the site. About an hour and a half in, I got another call. "Don't go to the site," Jerry said. "Come to the hospital."

I arrived a couple of hours later at the hospital in Fort Worth. Inside, the receptionist told me to take the elevator down to the ICU. As I was walking down the corridor to the waiting room, a couple of nurses pushing a gurney approached. There, on the table, was a body. That is the best way to describe it—it was the form of a person but so badly burned that I couldn't make out any defining features. Later I would learn that 60 percent of this man's body was covered by second- and third-degree burns.

I couldn't breathe. I leaned against the wall as the gurney passed, willing my heart rate to slow. Finally, from what felt like a great distance, I heard the district manager's voice.

"Jeet," he said. "Will you go talk to the welder's wife?"

I nodded. "Just give me a minute," I said. I took a deep breath and tried to compose myself. What could I possibly say to this woman? If she had seen him on the gurney as I had, there could be no doubt in her mind that her husband would be permanently disabled. I couldn't imagine what she was going through, what was running through her mind, how I could provide her with any comfort. I surely couldn't tell her that everything was going to be all right or claim that I could fix this—her life, her children's lives, and the life of her husband would never be the same.

Ten slow breaths later, I stood up straight and walked into the waiting room. Jerry was standing next to a young woman slumped in a chair, her head in her hands. I sat down in front of her. She looked up.

"I am so sorry," I said. I paused. Above us, the clock ticked on the wall. I swallowed, and cleared my throat. "I am so sorry," I repeated, "and I can't offer you anything more than these three things. Number one, I will make sure your husband gets the best possible medical care. Number two, I will make sure we find out exactly what happened. And number three, I give you my word that I will dedicate the rest of my life to making sure something like this never happens again."

What does it mean to **treat others with dignity and respect**? Those words get bandied about, and it can be difficult to pull them out of the realm of the philosophical and into reality, and to figure out what specific behaviors align with these values. For me, it starts with perspective, something tragedy tends to alter. I could have chosen to hang up the phone that early morning and go about the business of damage control without ever seeing the injured party. To be honest, on some of those sleepless nights after, a part of me wished I *had*. Driving out to see the welder was not an official duty, nor was it necessarily an expectation. But I did make that drive, and I am glad that I went to the hospital, because it offered me an opportunity to see my colleague who was injured, to express my support to the family, and, above all, learn one of the biggest lessons of my life.

To this day the image of him lying on the gurney, the image of his wife's shocked expression, stays with me. In that moment, it was impossible to reduce this employee, one out of many thousands across thirty countries, to just a number. He was a human being with an irrevocably damaged body and a family that would have to figure out a new survival plan. I would do whatever I could to make things, if not right, then at least as good as possible given the situation. I would make sure the welder and his family were taken care of. And I would do everything in my power to make sure something like that would never happen again.

The only way to do this was to get everyone on board. I'd been focused on safety from the start, and I'd thought we'd been doing a good job of it. Of course, we all agreed that safety was important. But intellectually agreeing with something, even signing papers or attending training on the topic, isn't the same as *knowing* at a deeper level why the more tedious tasks that this goal requires are worth the effort. In this instance, the welder had failed to properly isolate the part of the system on which he was working before he began, and so hydrocarbons broke loose and caught fire. The tasks required for keeping him safe were not complicated or difficult, which is probably the reason they were skipped—if we are not fully committed to paying attention to every single detail, then it's usually the mundane tasks that get overlooked. What could we do to remedy this? We needed to **engage hearts and minds**.

Though framed within the context of safety protocols, the following can apply not only to less dangerous fields but to other goals in life. In order to engage hearts and minds and treat others with dignity and respect, there are a few key things you must do.

TAKE RESPONSIBILITY

I was not the only one shaken up by this tragedy. The night after the accident, I couldn't help but replay that terrible scene in my mind. The next morning, my stomach in knots, I went into the office and met with the members of my leadership team. From the dark circles under my colleagues' eyes, I could tell that they hadn't slept very well either. Without wasting time on a formal greeting, I simply said, "Any human being who enters the premises has the fundamental right to go home safely to their family at the end of each shift, every day. We have to create a value system, a way to make sure every single one of our employees stays injury free. Safety will no longer be a priority; it will be a core value for us. Core values are nonnegotiable."

Now, the response could have gone a few different ways. I believe that there are a few gut reactions people tend to have in the face of crisis, tragedy, or simple error when culpability is involved. These are:

1. Sweep the incident under the rug.
2. Chock it up to coincidence, to being in the wrong place at the wrong time.
3. Blame the victim.
4. Turn a blind eye and pretend it never happened.
5. Take full responsibility and take whatever remedial action is necessary.

I had no doubt that everyone had the best of intentions. But not everyone had seen the welder as I had, and I wouldn't have been surprised had my team not wanted to think too hard about this individual or the situation as a whole. This was in the days before smartphones, when not just anyone could upload a mishap for the world to see, and it was easier to divert responsibility. We wouldn't have been the first company in history to brush our hands of an accident, or to go to great lengths to save face instead of taking the simpler path of admitting our failings. But we chose number five, swiftly and without argument.

That same day we set about hiring outside consultants to help us examine our practices and uncover our deficiencies. We basically opened our doors and said, "Come in and tell us what's wrong with us." It was not easy, but it was truly the only way to fix what was broken. Because how can you find a solution if you won't acknowledge a problem?

It became mandatory for Chevron Pipeline Company employees to ask "Why?" at least six times after a failure. Not only did this serve to expose weaknesses, it forced people to **get over failure**, to take action instead of sitting around moping, and to learn from mistakes and look forward. It also allowed us to trace the vulnerability all the way up the chain, rather than grabbing onto the easiest answer and assigning blame to those closest to the incident. For example, if a pump failed, we'd ask, "Why did the pump fail?" Answer: It was not lubricated according to the practice recommended by the manufacturer. "Why wasn't it lubricated?" Answer: The mechanic had too many tasks to complete. He is at capacity at fifteen tasks, but he was assigned twenty. "Why was the mechanic assigned too many tasks?" Answer: Because the refinery is understaffed, and his supervisor had to overload all employees. And so on. I would guess that 90 percent of the time, the root cause of an accident or wrongdoing was not intentional and, once people knew that their employers prioritized finding an answer over blaming and delivering punishment, they were more willing to investigate. Often, we found, there wasn't a single person who was to blame; rather, it was a broader issue that needed to be dealt with on multiple levels.

In a perfect world, we would see the signs of our vulnerabilities long before disaster struck. In a perfect world, we wouldn't need an explosion, a multi-plaintiff gender-discrimination lawsuit, or for a video of a CEO being belligerent to go viral in order see a problem and go about fixing it. This, however, is not a perfect world. So, when disaster strikes, the simplest route is to face it head-on and admit our mistakes.

This applies to the smaller obstacles in our lives, and our own behaviors that get in our way or cause other people harm. Ask yourself:

- How do you tend to deal with problems in your life? Do you tend to ignore them, blame others, put a spin on it? Or are you willing to take a close look and take responsibility?

HAVE A GOOD REASON

A welder knows how to use the correct welding rod, and how to complete the welding task in accordance with the prescribed procedure. They also know what safety gear to use—fire-retardant coveralls, goggles, fire-protective gloves, and the face shield and hard hat. All of these practices are clearly defined, and if you asked a welder to explain the best way to stay safe, they could probably recite the rules by rote. But whether or not they choose to follow them is another matter.

We have procedures and policies around how to perform each and every task safely. But if you ask someone who's been injured after skirting safety measures, they'll usually tell you that they knew what to do but chose not to, because of laziness or hurry or distraction. Let's say you come home from work and see that you have weeds growing up through the cracks in your walkway. This chore has been on your to-do list for weeks, and you know that it would make your partner happy if you would just go and take care of it already. You value your marriage and so you head over to the garage and get out the Weedwacker. Now, you know the safety goggles are around there somewhere, and that you should absolutely, without a doubt, wear them, but it'll take you an extra three or four minutes to find them, and you're tired and hungry, and you want nothing more than to go inside, crack open a beer, and lie down on the couch for a moment before you get up and start getting ready for dinner. So what do you do?

Someone with an engaged heart will ask:

1. What can go wrong? (Answer: the Weedwacker could hit a rock, which could fly up and hit me in the eye.)
2. What is the worst thing that can happen if something does go wrong? (Answer: I could be blinded in one eye. This will not only cause me great physical pain and create limitations in my vision, it will also take me out of work and put my family's well-being at risk.)
3. Am I doing everything I can to get this done safely? (Answer: I'm going to find those safety goggles.)

If you let tiredness or hunger override your sense, then you will go and cut those weeds, and put yourself at risk. If, however, you stop and consider the reasons for being safe, you are more likely to make the safe choice.

The consultants we hired helped us to implement the philosophy and methodology of the Incident and Injury Free (IIF) workplace, which focuses on trying to engage not just the minds but the hearts of people. The IIF principles are:

- Do it safely or not at all.
- There is always time to do it right.
- When in doubt, find out.

All Chevron employees were given a badge with the words "My reason for being safe" on one side and a plastic slot for keeping a photo on the other. Most people inserted a picture of their loved ones—of their significant others, their children and grandchildren, their dogs or cats. We also hung up huge family pictures along fences and entry gates. The idea was that, instead of following safety rules because they'd been told to or they feared punishment for not doing so, people would follow the safety rules because they had families to go home to, people who depended on them, or greater reasons for doing their work. It needed to be more than a mental exercise—their *hearts* needed to be in it.

This extends beyond the realm of safety. What if you stopped and considered *why* you take on life's big and small challenges, when it would be so much easier to cut corners? Why go to the effort of grocery shopping and cooking a nutritious meal when you could go to the drive-through and pick up a fast-food dinner? Why drive at the speed limit when you could get to your destination more quickly by speeding? Why read your child a bedtime story when you'd rather watch TV? Why bother going to work in the first place?

We need a good reason for managing our lives, one that accounts for the big picture, the far-ranging consequences of our actions and our long-term goals. Ask yourself: What is your reason?

FOCUS ON BEHAVIORS, NOT RESULTS

In the previous example, I recommended that, rather than focusing on how to get the job done as quickly as possible, you should follow safety protocols to a T, no matter how much you want to get inside so you can kick off your shoes and relax. In the same vein, I would suggest any gardener focus not on the results (clearing the weeds) but on the behavior itself (the action of clearing the weeds). This falls under the category of safety—if you are focused on your immediate actions and surroundings, you are less likely to make a careless mistake that could cause injury—as well as ensuring superior performance, because each and every individual behavior, when performed well, is the building block of a superior result.

This might sound obvious, but in fact this kind of performance management goes against the grain of conventional practices. In my experience, managers tend to get obsessed with results, and performance reviews often hinge on whether someone has met quarterly, semiannual, or annual targets. Of course, you must have a larger goal in mind as you work, but, in my experience, people respond better when their performance is measured by their level of productivity and the quality of their behaviors every day, not on overall output.

In short, managing behavior is the most effective way to manage performance. Here are a few important principles to effectively manage behavior:

1. **Understand the goal, communicate expectations clearly, and garner agreement before proceeding.**
   Setting unclear or vague goals that cannot be measured or realistically reached guarantees confusion and frustration. Effective goals start with a vision, a mission, and an outline of strategy. The goal itself must be SMART— Specific, Measurable, Achievable, Realistic, and Time-Based. SMART goals allow everyone to have a clear idea of the desired results while also breaking them down into approachable day-to-day tasks.

2. **Agree on metrics for measuring performance.** Like unclear goals, unclear or unarticulated metrics guarantee inefficiency and wasted effort. You must create metrics that are:

   - Clear and well-defined, so that people can use accessible data to understand how they can impact the goal
   - Focused on what is important
   - Aligned with the other units working in tandem
   - Consistently upheld, so that employees can stay on course without having to worry about a change in metrics

3. **Use well-articulated antecedents but emphasize consequences.** Antecedents are the things that come before a behavior, or the things that prompt a behavior by revealing expectations. Stop signs, for example, are antecedents for a driver to stop her car, and a ringing phone is an antecedent for answering the phone. Consequences are the events that occur following behaviors. All behaviors have consequences; for example, driving through a stop sign could have the negative consequence of causing a car accident, or answering the phone could have the positive consequence of getting to have a conversation with a friend. In the workplace, antecedents include job descriptions, business plans, or corporate policies which are designed to elicit certain behaviors from the workforce. Workplace consequences are bonuses, salary raises, promotions, as well as smaller monetary and nonmonetary awards that can give employees an added incentive. A simple "Thank You" written on a Post-it and left on an employee's desk has tremendous motivational impact. Negative consequences will stop a behavior but only for a period of time; when that punishment or other negative consequence disappears, the bad behavior is likely to return.

The theory of applied behavioral analysis posits that antecedents tend to have limited impact on behaviors. Usually they can help initiate a behavior, but more often than not an antecedent isn't enough to sustain it. Consequences are a much more effective tool, keeping people motivated for much longer—people will work with more focus and enthusiasm if they are working to earn a positive consequence. Good leaders constantly look for employees displaying good behaviors and reinforce them, instead of looking for mistakes. A mature organization delivers four or five times as many positive reinforcements as negative.

OPEN A FEEDBACK CHANNEL

Even with the safety badges and continual repetition of reasons for being safe, we knew that often the antecedents of policies and procedures were less effective than consequences, and that people tend to fall back on methods that expend the least amount of energy if not constantly monitored. The problem with the conventional means of monitoring was that it ran the risk of being perceived as an adversarial exercise between a supervisor and their staff, particularly when the feedback was framed in a negative way. Once an employee feels like there's an unbalanced power dynamic, there's a greater chance of them choosing to listen with only half an ear and then shrugging it off, or agreeing just to get the performance review over and done with. This, of course, is not engaging hearts and minds.

To deal with this, we implemented the Loss Prevention System, a behavior-based approach for improving safety which features a high degree of accountability. We focused on understanding the root causes of incidents and created nonhierarchical feedback loops by having peers and supervisors observe one another doing a task, focusing both on which behaviors were risky and which aligned with safety practices, and providing at least 80 percent positive feedback. We found that people were much more receptive when their successes were noted, followed by advice for how to do a good job even better. We found that effective feedback:

- Is delivered privately, nonjudgmentally, and in a timely fashion in a comfortable setting.
- Is constructive, not *de*structive, intended to help the individual succeed.
- Is clear, specific, and thorough.
- Uses real-life examples from the field and evidence-based information.
- Shows the impact of behaviors on goals and colleagues.
- Provides coaching, suggestions on how to improve performance, and the positive and negative consequences of altering performance.
- Involves empathic listening.
- Encourages and includes time for questions and further conversation.

The individual receiving feedback has certain responsibilities as well. These include:

- Asking for feedback with an objective to improve performance.
- Listening for understanding and for data.
- Asking clarifying questions to ensure feedback is NORMS-based (Not an interpretation, Observable, Reliable, Measurable, and Specific) and describes observation of the behavior and the effect.
- Separating base behavior from content. For example, if you want to encourage employees to express dissenting opinions, then you must listen to such expressions with composure and then truly consider them before accepting or dismissing them. You cannot shut down the content of the expression outright—this will have the effect of shutting down the behavior itself.

- Reinforcing the individual providing the feedback by soliciting coaching. Giving feedback is scary for many people and it does not take much to convince a person to stop giving feedback.
- Thanking the individual for the gift of feedback.

Every supervisor made a commitment to do a certain number of observations and review the observations done by others every month. Then, they would go and physically check to make sure the action items identified to remedy the situation had been implemented in the field. We also monitored goals using direct and third-party observation and feedback, data and information collection, employee surveys, and upward or 360 feedback. For the latter, an individual's subordinates, peers, and superiors were called upon to provide specific and constructive feedback by answering questions such as:

1. Describe the opportunity you have had to work with this person.
2. What specific contributions has this person made to the organization during the past year?
3. What constructive leadership behaviors has this person exhibited during the past year that have contributed to the organization's success?
4. What behaviors have you observed that have negatively impacted others?
5. What three specific behaviors would you like this person to continue to build on in the future?
6. What three specific behaviors would you like this person to stop doing in the future?
7. Do you have any other comments that would help this person become a more effective leader and enhance their contributions to the enterprise?

As President of Chevron Pipeline Company, I agreed to do my part and perform observations and provide feedback. Later in my career, when I was president of Chevron global manufacturing, I posted the results outside my office door and made them electronically available to all employees across the organization at all times, and, during our monthly leadership meeting, my advisor put all of our stats onscreen. After that there wasn't too much to say—if I had eight direct reports and only six fulfilled their commitments, that spoke for itself. It was as transparent a process as could be.

In 2002, right after my family and I moved to Australia, some friends arrived in town to visit. I drove them, in my new company-provided BMW, up to Blue Mountain for some sightseeing, and on the way back we stopped by a gas station to fill up the tank. It was my first time doing so with this particular vehicle, and I couldn't open the gas-tank lid. "I'll call the car dealership," I said, pulling my cell phone out of my pocket and beginning to dial. Then I heard a tapping on the pump station's glass window. I looked up. Behind the glass, the cashier was watching. She pointed at the phone and then wagged her finger and shook her head. I immediately turned it off and put it away.

The next day I sent her one hundred dollars and a card, in which I told her who I was and thanked her for calling me out on my unsafe behavior—using cell phones near gas pumps can cause fire through static electricity. In a moment of distraction, I'd gone for the fastest solution, one which put myself, my guests, and all bystanders at risk. I wasn't practicing what I was preaching, and I was grateful to her for her diligence.

Recently, my son Shammi and his wife, Melissa, came to visit me and Jan in Seattle. We were out at a restaurant and the service was terrible. Instead of skimping on the tip, I called over the manager to tell him about it. You see, giving feedback is a hard habit to let go of. Later, Shammi pointed out this enduring habit, recalling the time a flight attendant had given an alcoholic drink—a screwdriver, if memory serves—to his brother, who had been a minor at the time. I not only spoke frankly to the attendant about this error, I also wrote a letter to the airline to express my displeasure. But it's not just the negative experiences that elicit my feedback. Nowadays, I'm a big fan of Yelp and TripAdvisor. I don't just use it as a venue for venting my frustrations—I always give credit where it is due. I also always make a point of complimenting the people I come across in my daily life on a job well done.

Some may perceive this as nosy or intrusive, but I've found that it's a great way to make a connection and possibly contribute to someone's improvement. You might never find out there's an issue if everyone is too polite to bring it to your attention. This is why I believe that being open to feedback—both positive and negative—is essential for personal, professional, and communal development. Ask yourself:

- How often do you receive feedback? How do you feel about receiving feedback?
- How often do you give feedback? How do you feel about giving feedback?
- What are some ways you could develop your openness to both receiving and giving feedback?

ENCOURAGE CORRECT BEHAVIORS REGARDLESS OF CONTENT

Day in and day out, I went around reminding people that safety and reliability go hand in hand. On top of the safety badges and the Loss Prevention System reviews, every single one of Chevron's operators had been granted Stop Work Authority. This placed the responsibility for plant-wide safety in their hands and encouraged them to take the initiative to shut down the unit any time they saw something that was a major environmental or safety risk. Now, this was not a duty to be taken lightly—a plant shutdown, even a short one, can cost the company hundreds of thousands of dollars or more. But, after weighing the cost/risk benefits, we decided that we'd rather lose money than risk our employees' lives or the health of the community.

In the past, if an employee shut down a plant, we would have given them the third degree about why they'd made that decision. But with the Stop Work Authority in place, we had to reward that behavior no matter what, even when the shutdown turned out to be unjustified. One time, an operator at a refinery in Pembroke, Wales exercised his authority on a critical process unit. We could have gotten angry. We could have reprimanded him or fired him. Instead, we thanked him.

Two days later, I flew to the site and gave him the President's Award, which included $2,500. "You did the right thing," I told him.

This is an example of someone demonstrating a correct behavior and being rewarded for it even though, ultimately, the outcome may not have been desirable. Take this more common example: Let's say you want to encourage people to express their ideas. If you are committed to this, then you have to be open to whatever form that takes. If you're having a heated discussion with someone and they make an assertion without data to support it, you could summarily dismiss it, which would have the effect of discouraging this desired behavior. Instead, you could say something along the lines of "I appreciate you expressing your point of view, but I don't agree with your conclusion. Show me how the data supports your assertion." That encourages the behavior.

RECOGNIZE AND REWARD EXCELLENCE

After the Loss Prevention System was in place, I vowed that, if a refinery were able to go for one full year without an incident, my colleagues from the leadership team and I would visit the location to personally cook and serve a meal, and clean up afterwards. I fulfilled this promise at many locations over several years. While the crew was eating the tandoori chicken or barbecue we had prepared, we would stand up and **say thank you** for their exemplary work.

A thank-you can go a long way. If you can afford it, I recommend giving more tangible rewards as well. At Chevron, we implemented a Recognition and Award Program to identify and recognize outstanding contributions. There were four tiers of rewards:

- Tier 4: **The R&A Closet**. Employees were encouraged to recognize and award (R&A) one another—at Chevron Pipeline Company, we had a closet filled with small gift items, and employees could go in and, after noting in the register whom they were thanking and why, take a baseball cap or a mug to give to them to show their gratitude.

- Tier 3: **Supervisor Award**. Employees could submit nominations to an R&A committee to review. The committee would select the deserving candidates and award them gift certificates for dinner for two at a local steakhouse, a weekend at a nearby resort, or cash, usually between $50 and $500. Every now and then they would award up to $1,000.
- Tier 2: **The President's Award**. This award was reviewed and recommended by the same committee. If an employee's action made a significant contribution, they would get up to $10,000 or more. I personally presented each of these awards.
- Tier 1: **The Chairman's Award**. If someone or a team did something absolutely exceptional, I would personally review and recommend the person or team for this award, which started at $25,000.

BENCHMARK AGAINST THE BEST

When I joined Caltex in Australia, the company was on the verge of bankruptcy; it had lost over $130 million in the year prior and had a debt ratio well above 60 percent. It was dying by a thousand small cuts, by systemic inefficiency and imprudent spending. So it wasn't all that difficult to **make the business case for change**. It was simple: if we didn't, the business would fail and we'd all lose our jobs.

That knowledge, however, didn't necessarily make the changes themselves easy. Change is uncomfortable for everybody, no matter how necessary. I told my team as much. I also showed them a cartoon of an Iditarod race, with a row of huskies pulling a sled. The caption read, "If you are not the lead dog, the scenery never changes." We needed to set our sights not just on pulling ourselves out of debt, but also on no longer accepting our place as a bottom-tier performer, or always operating in survival mode. "If you're not the lead dog," I said, "then you'll always be looking at the next dog's rear end. We need to be the lead dog."

I will admit that I had an obsession with being the best, one that carried over into my personal life in perhaps unhealthy ways. I have been driven my whole life, driven to succeed and achieve, and it's hard for me to relax my standards when the situation warrants it. I remember coaching my eldest son, Amby's, soccer team, and how focused I was on winning. I pushed those kids hard. True, the team won the championship every year. But those kids also saw me yelling and screaming at the refs. Once I got a red card and had to leave—I distinctly remember the embarrassed look on Amby's face as I walked off the field. I regret that I forgot that the game was just a game, and I was so focused on winning that I forgot that the kids were just kids and we were there not *just* to win but to have fun.

Shammi and Amby in their soccer uniforms.

But in no way do I regret my obsession with being the best within the context of my profession. It was not enough for us to judge our performance against the industry average and settle for reaching the middle of the pack. That kind of low expectation doesn't serve to rally the troops. Instead, nothing less than the best would be good enough.

And so we cut costs. We optimized labor levels, reduced perks and travel companywide, and negotiated with our suppliers, contractors, and customers to set up a system that would allow money to flow more easily. We talked to investors in Boston, New York, Chicago, and beyond, ultimately raising more than double our initial goal to keep the organization afloat. We talked to franchisees to learn how we could improve, budgeted for advertising, improved safety and reliability by implementing the Incident and Injury-Free Culture. Everyone made sacrifices. But, more importantly, everyone reaped the rewards.

The only way to reach the front of the pack is to reward excellence *and* engage the hearts and minds of everyone on your team—you must do both. As soon as the company got out of the red and into the black, I spoke to the board about giving a small number of company shares to all employees, irrespective of position. The board granted my request, and overnight the entire Caltex team became shareholders. Now they would directly feel the impact of their performance. This is another way to **engage hearts and minds**—the employees now had a real reason for striving. Instead of gathering around the water cooler for gripe sessions, people talked about their shares, and actions they could take to make them go up. In town hall meetings across the country, I presented the results of their hard work, the improvement in the company's financial performance. Congratulatory displays weren't a big part of Australian culture, but I wanted to make sure the moment was noted and celebrated. I remember one town hall meeting in Sydney, where I said, "I want you all to stand up." The auditorium was filled with the sound of squeaking chairs as all three hundred employees got to their feet. "Please do me the favor of turning to the person to your right," I continued, "the person to your left, the person in front of you, and the person behind you. Shake hands and thank them for their contribution." Once they had, I said, "Now I want you to join me in giving one another the biggest round of applause ever given."

Jeet, as Elvis, singing "Jailhouse Rock" with Running on Empty, Caltex
Australia's in-house band, at the company holiday party.

Stock prices went up four or five times in the next fifteen months. For the financial year of 2002–2003, Caltex Australia saw the highest gains in share price on the Australian Stock Exchange. We were in the newspaper constantly, not for unfounded allegations but for our successes. The morale went from being the worst I'd ever seen to going through the roof. And we became the leader of the pack.

Our worst failures can bring about our greatest triumphs, if we are willing to take responsibility for our mistakes and dedicate ourselves to learning from them. The accident outside of Fort Worth was absolutely horrible, and it goes without saying that my colleagues and I wish it had never happened. No one should have to experience that pain and suffering. But it did teach us a valuable lesson: If you don't engage hearts and minds, you allow for half measures and sloppy work. **If you don't recognize and reward excellence, you will breed mediocrity.** And if you do have a good reason, you will be able to give your best effort to not just achieve, but to make it home safe and sound at the end of the day.

CHAPTER 6

NEGOTIATE EFFECTIVELY

I was driving on Interstate 5 toward Seattle when I got the call on my old, brick-size cell phone. We were on vacation—Jan was sitting beside me in the passenger seat and Amby and Shammi were in the back listening to their Walkmans and looking out the windows.

"You need to come back," my boss said. "You'll be leaving on Monday for Kazakhstan."

In 1993, Chevron reached an agreement with Kazakhstan to develop and produce oil from the Tengiz oil field, located on the northeast corner of the Caspian Sea in Kazakhstan. To the east lies Uzbekistan and Turkmenistan; to the south lies Iran; to the west is Azerbaijan and Georgia. And, to the north, Russia stakes its more than six-million-square-mile claim. The Druzhba Pipeline, the only existing pipeline at the time, had begun its transport of crude oil from this region in the mid-1960s and, not only was it controlled by the Russians, it was already running close to its capacity. Meaning that billions of barrels of oil were landlocked—stuck between these countries and inaccessible to the rest of the world.

In order to monetize this asset, we would have to find creative ways to get the oil to the world market.

In 1995, I was assigned by Chevron to explore the alternatives. By this time, a Dutch promoter—in collaboration with the Russian Federation, Republic of Kazakhstan, and the Sultanate of Oman—had floated a project that involved construction of a pipeline from the Tengiz field to the Russian port of Novorossiysk on the Black Sea through the Russian territory. The oil would then be loaded on ships in Novorossiysk for a journey through the strait of Bosporus in Turkey, out to the Mediterranean Sea, and then west to the world markets.

When I arrived on the scene, I focused my attentions on the organizations interested in the pipeline project, a list which had grown to include—along with the Russian Federation, the Republic of Kazakhstan, and Sultanate of Oman—the oil companies Mobil, Oryx, British Gas, Agip, KazMunayGas, Rosneft, Transneft, and Lukoil. After some deliberation, the Western oil companies selected Chevron to lead the negotiations on their behalves, primarily because of Chevron's large holdings in the Tengiz field. As the leader of Chevron's project team, I was saddled with the responsibility of negotiating a deal in service to the diverse interests of all stakeholders.

It'd be an understatement to say that not everyone in the industry was on the same page. First, the Western companies would need to find some basic alignment before approaching the three sovereign nations, each of which were bringing their own agendas to the table. To complicate matters further, we didn't all speak the same language, not just metaphorically but literally as well. All negotiations would have to be interpreted from English into Russian and vice versa, which would both slow the process and make it difficult, through inadvertent and intentional misrepresentation, for the parties to truly understand one another's positions.

The first time I met Energy Minister Shafranik, a traditional Soviet-era leader, I said that, with joint effort, we should be able to find a "win-win" solution for all parties involved. Minister Shafranik leaned forward, his face turning a shade that would put a tomato to shame.

"Mr. Bindra," he said, just inches from my face, "there is no such thing as 'win-win.' If you win, I lose. And I do not know how to lose."

This was not the ideal way to start a new assignment, and it was clear from the start that this would not be an ordinary undertaking. This, it appeared, would be more like a battle between adversaries. And so I rallied the troops.

Because of the complexity of the language and cultural barriers, I assembled a diverse team of people who could assess the situation from multiple angles. Irwin Lichtblau was the top-notch business analyst from Chevron, Ed Chow was a very knowledgeable public- and government-affairs professional, and Rob James represented our interests as legal counsel. (Craig Rice, another business analysist, would come in later.)

It wasn't too difficult to find those first three members, but it took some time for us to identify a Russian professional who could act as my coach. Eventually we identified Natasha Novoselova and hired her to be our expert on Russia and my mentor. Not only was she an intelligent and charismatic person in her own right, she was also the daughter of a Russian ambassador and so had been exposed to forging diplomatic relations from a young age. She knew how business was conducted in the Russian Federation. Her knowledge and insight would prove to be invaluable.

Though the team was ready to go, negotiations did not begin for almost six months. In Russia, rapport was considered essential, and there were no shortcuts or timesavers when creating a positive dynamic between the many negotiators. And so, while we built new relationships, we also did our homework.

Negotiating is an integral part of our day-to-day life. Deciding on where to go to dinner with your spouse is negotiation, as is getting your child to make her bed in the morning, though you're probably not going to ask your loved ones to sign a contract to bring about the end of a discussion. Similar principles do apply when determining the parameters of a project with a colleague or discussing salary and benefits with a potential employee, however, and ultimately it's about the effort it takes to reach a mutual agreement through dialogue. How can you be the best negotiator you can be?

ESTABLISH RAPPORT

Never underestimate the value of breaking bread. Whether you are in Oslo or Cape Town, Kentucky or Tokyo, breaking bread is a bonding ritual essential for breaking down barriers, understanding one another's motivations, and establishing trust. It became evident that this getting-to-know-you period was very important to the Russians, and that it would be in our best interests to not hurry this process. We simply could not expect to fly into Moscow on a Monday and return to San Francisco on Friday with a major business agreement.

So we spent the first six months getting to know the key players from the Russian Federation, the Republic of Kazakhstan, and the Sultanate of Oman through regular social meetings. The new pipeline was off the conversational table, and any talk of cutting a deal was verboten; instead, we set about getting to know our counterparts on a personal level. It took a few months just to reach a point where we could comfortably address one another by first name, and embrace instead of shaking hands. At breakfasts and cocktail hours and dinners that lasted into the dark hours of the night, we learned the details of one another's families, discussed current events, and went over the results of the latest tennis matches. Those Russians really loved tennis. I learned their favorite wines and what they liked to eat for breakfast. I must admit that I consumed more vodka in those six months than I had in my entire life prior to this assignment.

In September of that first year, in 1995, Jan joined me on a visit to the Republic of Georgia. Upon our return to St. Petersburg, we were told that the air traffic controllers had gone on strike and all flights to Moscow were canceled. I'd learned that, when stuck in a foreign airport, your best bet is to find a younger person, because they will be more likely to speak English. This turned out to be correct, and the young woman we'd asked suggested that we go to the railway station to catch an overnight train to Moscow instead.

We arrived at seven o'clock in the morning the following day, well rested after a night in a private, comfortable compartment. We rushed to our hotel for quick showers, then got in the waiting vehicle of our host, the minister of energy. We started toward Vladimir, Russia's capital during the Middle Ages. At around 9:30 a.m., the minister pulled out a chilled bottle of champagne and popped the cork. "Happy birthday, Mr. Bindra," he said in his accented English, toasting the day that had passed a week earlier. That was the first of many toasts in what would turn out to be a very long and drunken visit.

Soon we arrived at the outskirts of Vladimir to find the mayor and his entourage, who escorted us to the city hall, where he opened a bottle of top-shelf vodka. Any toast to the nation or the family requires a bottoms up from every man present, and I believe we had three toasts in total, followed by some light snacks. Then we went on to the historic town of Suzdal for a sightseeing tour, where we celebrated approximately six more toasts with that city's mayor. As you can imagine, we were feeling pretty tipsy by that time. At around five o'clock in the afternoon, we arrived at an old monastery, where a banquet hall had been set with a long table that could easily accommodate the thirty or so people who'd joined our tour. Once we'd all taken our seats, the mayor of Suzdal stood up.

"Today I request everyone in attendance to do a toast," he said. "Usually we make an exception for women, but today they must also do a toast." And so we went around the table, with each person giving a speech and raising their glass.

Now, Jan tends to be very shy, and she usually hates public speaking of any kind. On that day, however, she'd had plenty of alcohol to calm her nerves. When her turn came, she got to her feet with only a small wobble or two. "A toast!" she shouted, barely slurring the words. For the next ten minutes, with much exuberant hand gesturing, Jan delivered the toast of a lifetime.

That wasn't the last toast of the night—we had another cognac toast on our way out of the city, as well as pierogis eaten on the side of the pitch-dark road by a cornfield—but it was certainly the most memorable.

In the end we forged friendships with key players that transcended the Caspian Pipeline Project—many of us became friends for life. Still, I had to work to maintain my patience. But, ultimately, this long interlude was a blessing in disguise, because these informal conversations allowed us to forge a bond, develop trust, dispel tension, and, most of all, learn about the other negotiators' styles and manners.

Do you tend to skip the critical ritual of breaking bread in order to speed up a negotiation? If so, I recommend that you slow things down. Though establishing rapport might not feel directly relevant to the task at hand, I can assure you that it is, and that doing so can only help you in your efforts. Out of all the lessons in this book, this one is perhaps the most fun to implement. Here's how.

- Never neglect the niceties. As you would when meeting people in your personal life, spend some time making chitchat and getting to know the person on the other side of the table or phone line before you get to work.
- Don't be in a hurry. Aggressively pushing an agenda right from the get-go can be off-putting, and it can make you seem desperate. So know where you want to go, but take your time getting there.
- Meet outside of the office. Though you can break bread in a business setting, talking in a less formal atmosphere, like a restaurant, coffee shop, or at a baseball game can do wonders for creating ease and sparking conversation.

IDENTIFY THE STAKEHOLDERS AND DECISION MAKERS

The first thing I did when I arrived in Russia was to refuse to meet with the Dutch promoter who had originally floated the project. He had suggested that Chevron fund the entire project, while he would retain 25 percent interest in the project as a promoter's fee. This, as you might guess, was unacceptable from a commercial point of view. After a thorough review of his file, I concluded that he had done nothing beyond wheeling and dealing, coming up with schemes and making connections, and that meeting with him would only serve to legitimize him and include him as a credible stakeholder, something I was not willing to do. Instead, I focused on figuring out who really held the power.

It is often not possible to have all decision makers, stakeholders, and influencers at the table. As I mentioned in chapter 2, getting to know the people with whom you'll be working directly is essential, and, while you do, you should also learn as much as you can about those who are pulling the strings behind the scenes. Discover what authority rests with the negotiator and where the source of greater authority lies. Is there a committee or an individual whom the negotiator will be returning to every day or week? If so, get to know them and their position as best you can.

At the same time, make sure the other negotiators know who has your back. For example, we involved the European Bank for Reconstruction and Development (EBRD), a significant influencer in the region, as a potential financier of the project, which helped us prove our legitimacy. We also presented our story to as many stakeholders as possible and spent a tremendous amount of effort educating bureaucrats and politicians at all levels of the Russian Federation, Republic of Kazakhstan, and Sultanate of Oman so that they knew where we were coming from and what resources we were drawing on.

SET ORGANIZATIONAL GOALS

As a negotiator, you need to be very clear as to what entails a good outcome for you. If you have loyalty to other groups, as I did with the Western energy companies during this negotiation, then you must also understand the strategic goals of not only your own company, but other stakeholders as well. Have frequent conversations with your team and the others involved so that you can clearly and confidently articulate your goals once you get to the negotiation table. Ask yourself:

- What is a desirable outcome on each negotiation issue?
- What are the absolute must-haves?
- Where are we willing to compromise, and what would we want in return?
- What is our walk-away point for each critical issue?

Be aware that, as you learn more about the other side or sides, your goals will likely evolve. Identify potential alternatives for each issue and clearly understand which are acceptable to you on a standalone basis and which are acceptable in combination with other business parameters.

IMAGINE THE OTHER SIDE'S IDEAL OUTCOME

You won't have all the information necessary to fully understand the must-haves of the other side, but you must take the time to step into their shoes so that you can make an educated guess about their business drivers. For example, casual conversations over shots of vodka revealed that the key negotiator from Russia—who came from Transneft, the organization that managed the myriad of oil and gas pipelines in the area—wanted to manage both building the pipeline *and* the operations after construction, while the Russian Federation wanted to maintain control over movement of hydrocarbons from the region. I spent many hours chatting with Anatoly Shalatov, Russia's deputy minister of fuel and energy and the final decision maker, over hot tea. Whenever I went to his office, he would say "Chai or coffee?" before getting down to the business at hand. Informal lunches and dinners—breaking bread—offer unique opportunities to get a glimpse of the other side's motivations and, over time, allow a picture of their interests to emerge. Ask yourself:

- What's in it for the individual negotiator? Recognition, promotion, building an empire?
- What's in it for the organization? Enhanced revenue, greater influence, more control?
- What's in it for other stakeholders?

DETERMINE ACCEPTABLE COMPROMISES

A good negotiator spends time identifying areas of common ground, options for compromise, and which issues could be effectively traded to gain advantage. When we learned that the Russian Federation wanted a large share of pipeline ownership without putting any money into the project, we had good reason to want to walk away from the deal. But, frankly, the pipeline had to traverse through Russian territory and so we had to accept that we were in a weaker position. We asked ourselves: Where could we cede incremental value while still holding on to our most important goals? How would we prove that our requests were fair and reasonable? To make our case, we reviewed many multi-partner projects and gathered information about the commercial models used for them. This enabled us to insist that the ownership in the project reflect the contributions made by the parties involved. It also allowed us to see what had been acceptable for those who came before us, and to use that to understand where there might be room to move and where we would have to stand our ground.

In order to make your own case, assemble external benchmarks. This could be deals done in the past, salary figures for people with the same amount of experience or with the same job titles, protocols used in companies you've worked for previously, etc. If you are new in your career or transitioning into a new project or role, this will help you to paint a more detailed picture of what to expect. Not only will this prepare you to come to the table with concrete examples to serve as evidence, it will also give you insight into what is reasonable and what is not when your counterpart makes an offer.

**

We'd done our homework, getting to know the people with whom we were working, outlining our goals, and studying the situation from as many angles as we could. And yet, when it came time to sit down and sort through the issue, we found our mode of operation and that of the Russian negotiators incompatible, nearly to the point of being insurmountable. The process unraveled over the course of two long and difficult years, with many stutter steps, stalls, and setbacks along the way. For the duration, I made approximately seventy trips between the Bay Area, London, and Moscow. Sometimes, I'd be home for no more than forty-eight hours, barely enough time to change clothes, read my sons a book before bedtime, and kiss my wife goodbye before heading out the door again. My discomfort was not an unfortunate side effect of international dealmaking; rather, it was part and parcel of the Russians' negotiation tactics. To say that we'd brought a knife to a gun fight isn't accurate—it was more like we'd shown up expecting a boardroom and discovered a hall of mirrors.

In the beginning, the representatives from the Russian Federation and the Sultanate of Oman told us that they'd already spent close to $75 million on the project and therefore deserved financial credit for that investment as part of the deal. When the Chevron team asked for proof of the work product, we were given the runaround. And so we began investigating where this money had gone if, in fact, it had been spent at all.

When in Moscow, I stayed at the Metropol Hotel, and my habit was to get up at 7:15 a.m., pick up a newspaper, and read it over a breakfast of blini or house-made yogurt and granola in the hotel restaurant. One morning—a few months after we'd finally begun formal negotiations, in 1996—as I was locking the door to my room, a man approached me in the hallway. It was just me and him and a row of closed doors, no sounds of life except for the distant hum of traffic.

"Do I know you?" I asked when it became clear that he'd come to see me.

"You don't know me," he said in English with a strong Russian accent, "but I know you."

I swallowed and waited for whatever came next.

"I have a serious message to convey to you," the man continued. "Your line of questioning could reflect poorly on important people. We want you to abandon it."

"Excuse me," I said, stepping past him and walking away down the hall.

"I wouldn't do that. You're the only wage earner in your family, aren't you? I wouldn't do something that they would regret."

I stopped, turned, and looked him right in the eye. "I don't know you. Why should I listen to you?"

"I'm not speaking metaphorically, Mr. Bindra," he replied. "This could be devastating to you and your family."

I stared at him, unbelieving.

"Let me convince you. This trip, you arrived on Flight 437. You landed at 17.15. Sasha was waiting for you in the car outside customs."

He recited the license plate number, then went on. "You checked in and went to your room, put your suitcase down, washed your face and brushed your teeth, then went downstairs to the restaurant, where you ordered *melanzane parmigiana* and a decaf cappuccino." He then noted the color of my underclothes to underline his point.

This was not the only time my team would realize that we'd been followed, listened to, or had our rooms searched. We'd been warned not to give any gift not sanctioned by Chevron or have one-on-one interactions, however innocent, with Russian women, for fear of blackmail. Every single time we needed to call our superiors in California, corporate security had to arrange a different car to drive us to a different business to use their phone. One time, a colleague was visiting me in my suite and saw that one of the paintings was tilted. When he got up to straighten it, he discovered a couple of wires poking out of the wall. Fifteen minutes after he pulled them out, the hotel phone rang. It was the manager, calling to let us know that we would need to leave the room so his repairman could perform some routine maintenance.

Eventually, after I received another veiled threat—this time at Hyde Park in London on a sunny afternoon—my colleague Irwin Lichtblau tried to convince me to wear a bulletproof vest. I didn't like the idea and never went for it. Our security team told us: "Don't walk alone. Don't go out after dark. Get in cars only if you know the driver. Don't use the hotel phone to call the United States." Later, Kazakhstan's minister of oil and gas approached me after a meeting in Almaty, the capital of Kazakhstan, to let me know that my life was in danger, and to suggest that I ramp up our security further.

All of this was quite unnerving—which, of course, was the intention. The intimidation tactics didn't end once we got to the negotiations, and over time and with careful study, my team compiled a list of methods used by the Russians. We even had little laminated cards made up to carry with us, which included these notes:

1. Carefully plan all important meetings in advance and when they are underway stage manage the proceedings to one's own advantage.

2. Divert attention to minor points to delay consideration of major issues under dispute and to wear down one's opponent.

3. Adhere (but only when convenient) to the letter of agreements, ignoring completely the underlying intent.

4. Maintain a selective memory for facts, referring only to those which support one's own position.

5. Never allow your opponent to implement his own strategies and plans for the meeting.

6. Never accept that discussion on a matter is closed if the outcome during previous considerations was not favorable to one's position.

7. Stay focused on having one's own way—whatever it may cost.

8. Make occasional use of emotional outbursts to shock and frighten opponent.

9. Operate on the premise that the best defense is a good offense.

10. Refer to protocols and documents long ago superseded to reopen points for discussion.

11. Generally ignore all arguments counter to one's position and give no indication of being susceptible to arguments based on simple logic and fact.

12. Exploit and take maximum advantage of any errors, however trivial, made by one's opponent.

13. Attack on many fronts simultaneously to keep opponent off balance.

14. Spring surprises at appropriate times to disrupt the proceedings.

15. Resort to outright lies when required, but only if the risk of detection is low (this condition is optional).

16. Make use of powerful allies and encourage them to apply pressure both in and out of the meeting.

17. Sow the seeds of confusion in regard to points under discussion to obscure the facts.

18. When the discussion is going against one's position, arrange for an interruption or simply walk out, claiming urgent need elsewhere.

Understanding how the Russians thought and worked was critical to our operation, and it helped us to gain clarity on our own values and practices when it came to negotiation. Here is what I would recommend you do the next time you find yourself at the table.

ESTABLISH THE GROUND RULES

Right from the start, all parties must agree to the basic parameters. Make decisions about processes—and don't forget to write them down! Ask the group:

- When will we meet?
- How long will the meetings last?
- Who will speak for either side?
- How will the decisions be documented?
- Will there be interim agreements, or will all issues need to be resolved before any agreement is signed?

LISTEN ACTIVELY AND SEEK OPEN COMMUNICATION

A good negotiator is a master listener. Natasha Novoselova, our team's Russia expert and my mentor, interpreted not just what was said but the body language of the Russian negotiators and told us what might be the actual intent behind the words. She also helped us to frame our responses in a manner that would be received more favorably by the Russians. This was a critical component of the eventual success of these negotiations. To listen actively:

- Keep your attention focused on the speaker. Look for signals coming out of body language. For the most part, these are similar across cultures. For example, sitting back in the chair with arms crossed usually means skepticism or frustration, smiling and nodding with eyebrows raised means excitement or agreement, and looking away while scratching the head or squinting usually connotes concentration.

- Take notes as appropriate.
- Ask open-ended questions to learn more about the speaker's intent, concerns, and objectives.
- Do not formulate your response until the speaker is finished and you have had a chance to collect your thoughts.
- Repeat what you heard to give the other side confidence that you have listened to them.
- Express empathy for the other side's perspective and concerns.
- Acknowledge mistakes. In long, drawn-out negotiations mistakes are bound to happen. Acknowledge them and address them promptly before they get cast in concrete and cannot be reversed.
- Seek feedback and probe for understanding. Take every opportunity in and out of the negotiating forum to communicate your views and seek feedback from the other side as well as your own team. Address the feedback as appropriate and adjust your strategy going forward.
- Look for commonalities. Catch points of agreement and build upon them. Each agreement is a building block for a consensus.

MAINTAIN YOUR COMPOSURE

As displayed by our team's long list of Russian tactics, we'd quickly become aware that the negotiators wouldn't hesitate to use every technique possible to intimidate and distract us from the issue. Occasionally they resorted to calling names and pounding tables. At one point they forced us to negotiate from 10:00 a.m. until 9:00 p.m. every day for twenty-eight days in a row, during which we were offered only cookies, soft drinks, tea, or coffee for sustenance. They requested that each day's discussion be documented overnight, including translation into Russian. We received threats to our lives, my room was wiretapped, and we were constantly followed. I can only hope that you will never have to face such adverse circumstances. But no matter the situation, staying calm is always the best approach. Our method of maintaining composure was based on the following principles:

- Don't let the other side bully you, and never resort to personal attacks. Always keep personal issues separate from business issues. Even under great pressure, stick to the issue at hand.
- Maintain a sense of humor. The Russian team's creative obfuscations became something of a joke among those of us from the West, and when we weren't overwhelmed by frustration we found it comedic. This outlook helped us to keep calm and steer the discussions back to business issues.
- Acknowledge the difficulty of an issue if you see the other side's negotiator becoming tense.
- Request a caucus if you are not sure of the direction of negotiations. Consult your team members.
- If you reach an impasse—including reaching the point of exhaustion—and do not seem to be making any progress, ask for a cooling-off period. Regroup with your team and adjust your strategy. The other side will probably do the same.
- Use silence as a weapon. Don't be too anxious to respond to the other side's comments. It makes an inexperienced negotiator nervous and she may start negotiating with herself. You may end up receiving some concessions.

ENSURE PROPER APPROVALS

It is important to understand who is making the decision—an individual or a committee—and if that person or group is present at the table.

You have full rights to firmly and politely request their participation in the process. Don't hesitate to ask:

- Who will make the decision on this issue?
- What is the process that will be used to make the decision on your side?

Keep in mind that, if you do meet the ultimate decision maker, you can expect that they will try to extract some more concessions, so make sure that you have left yourself some room. When you *do* make concessions of any kind, be sure to make a big deal out of it. I used to say things like, "This is an important issue, and I am making a compromise only because I want to get the job done." Be explicit about it, otherwise it will go unnoticed.

Clearly know the scope of your own authority, and don't be hesitant to kick the issue to higher levels when appropriate. This also allows you to extract more value when the next level from your side gets involved.

It is essential that specific clauses that require authority beyond those at the negotiating table are legally approved by those who have the authority to do so. In our case we had to request a special decree by the Russian president and approval by the Russian Duma (parliament) to ensure that the terms would be enforceable.

KNOW WHEN TO STOP . . . AND DOCUMENT EVERYTHING

A few months before we signed the official agreement, Russian President Boris Yeltsin flew in from China for the ceremony. It was eleven o'clock in the morning when he arrived completely fall-down drunk. (Kazak President Nursultan Nazarbayev and I were completely stand-up sober.) President Yeltsin had to hold on to the podium as he gave his remarks, and he had to be escorted out before he could finish. Still, it was a proud moment because it marked the huge strides we had made toward our goal.

Signing ceremony for the first protocol in the presence of President
Yeltsin of Russia and Kazakhstan President Nazarbayev.

As negotiations proceed it is very likely that you will reach agreement on several issues. Don't keep debating the issue past an agreement by the other side. Often, inexperienced negotiators keep debating well beyond the point of useful conclusion, and end up reopening the issue. When you reach an agreement on an issue that meets your needs, quickly summarize the terms, jointly document them and, if possible, sign the agreement and celebrate the progress. We signed several protocols during the life of the negotiations, celebrating each signing as progress. This builds trust and gives hope to both sides.

In a prolonged negotiation with multiple issues, it is recommended that you request both parties initial the agreement for the issue at hand. Once agreements are reached on multiple issues, you must regularly review them in totality to make sure that they collectively make sense. Occasionally an issue may have to be revisited as it conflicts with subsequent agreements. Err on the side of caution by building mechanisms into the agreement that will enhance your ability to enforce the terms. For example, at one point we reached an agreement only to find out that the Russian Federation had changed the fiscal regime during its implementation. We were forced to add a clause in the agreement that ensured compensation, garnered from the benefits designed to flow to the Russian Federation, for any subsequent changes in fiscal regime.

At the end of a negotiation, look at the business from a holistic perspective to ensure it all fits together before inking a deal. With your team, capture lessons learned, such as:

- Was the preparation adequate?
- What worked well?
- What did not work? Why?
- How did the roles work out for the negotiating team?
- What can be done to improve for the future?
- What training could have helped? What training should be provided for the future?
- Can a checklist be developed to ensure nothing is missed?

Then celebrate!

We signed the official agreement in the presidential palace in Almaty. It had been a drawn-out and tense venture, which made our success all the sweeter. We'd managed to negotiate with three sovereign nations and a handful of oil companies to bring about the construction of a nearly one-thousand-mile pipeline that would transport millions of tons of crude oil to the world market. This was to be one of my most memorable experiences, and one of my career's crowning achievements.

Most of the negotiations you get into will probably not be as embattled as my negotiations with the Russians. Hopefully you will never have to deal with eleven-hour days, abusive counterparts, or stalkers threatening violence. Even in the friendliest negotiation, however, you will need to take the time to get to know who you are working with and the details of their agenda. You will also need to understand your own limitations and sticking points, when to stick to your guns and when to back down. I do not believe that negotiation has to be a zero-sum game, but the better prepared you are, the more likely you are to win.

CHAPTER 7

HOLD THE HIGHEST STANDARDS

The day after I arrived in Australia, in 2002, to take over the job of managing director and CEO of Caltex Australia Ltd, the *Sydney Morning Herald* ran a story with the headline "Raids on 'Price Fixing' Petrol Giants" on the front page. It was accompanied by a photograph of official-looking men, their arms loaded with boxes, walking out of Caltex's headquarters. The article described how Australia's antitrust watchdog group, the Australian Competition and Consumer Commission (ACCC), had raided the offices of Mobil, Shell, and Caltex, claiming that these companies were keeping prices artificially high, along with other noncompetitive behaviors.

That was quite the welcome. I'd known before agreeing to the job that the company was in bad shape—that was the primary reason I'd been brought in. The corporate executive vice president had told me, "We want you as CEO, but you have to understand that Caltex Australia is on the verge of bankruptcy. You might just end up moving to Australia to wind the business down. There's a good chance you'll be back in six months." His warning did not deter me. Part of the reason I took the job was that Jan was thrilled about the prospect of living in Australia, and part was that I am not one to turn down a challenge.

I was fully prepared for a bumpy road ahead—but I certainly wasn't prepared for nationwide public scrutiny from day one.

The day after that headline splashed across the *Sydney Morning Herald*'s front page, on April 25, 2002, I got a call from Australia's version of the *Today Show*, asking for an interview. I hadn't even learned my direct reports' names, let alone the greater complexities of the business! But what else could I do but agree?

I spent the entire night with the general affairs manager, preparing for the interview. It was a long, nerve-wracking night, and a shower and a cup of coffee in the morning didn't give me the confidence boost I needed. I would just have to do the best I could on no sleep and with limited intel.

The interview was not what anyone would call friendly. "What do you think about the accusation that Caltex has engaged in anticompetitive behavior?" the host asked in various ways.

"Listen," I kept repeating, "I just arrived. I don't know what's going on yet. I can guarantee you that we are doing a thorough investigation. And if we find something, I promise that we will admit it."

The interviewer continued, "What do you think of the Australian Competition and Consumer Commission?"

"I believe competition is good for Caltex, it is good for the industry, and, above all, it is good for Australia," I replied.

Afterward, I went to the office and called in our chief legal counsel and the heads of operations, marketing, finance, and public affairs. We sat down around the big table in the conference room—I could tell that these important members of my team were nervous by the subtle ways in which they were fidgeting. I let a few moments of silence pass, then looked around the table, making eye contact with each one in turn before asking, "Do you know if we have participated in something unethical or illegal?" In turn, they each said no. "OK," I said. "But that is not enough. We will need to obtain independent counsel, and we will need to question *everyone*. We need to see if we have a rogue employee in our midst."

Every day for the next seven or eight weeks, this group gathered to share updates and developments. From the ACCC we got nothing but radio silence as they combed through our seized documents. Finally, the independent counsel gave us their assessment: they hadn't found anything to be concerned about.

Soon thereafter, we received word that the ACCC was going to drop the charges.

For all that time, the *Sydney Morning Herald* had been running stories about the situation, including a cartoon of me with watchdogs nipping at my heels. Now, I told my team, "When they started the investigation, the newspapers had it splashed in big bold letters across

Watchdog nipping at Jeet's heels, published by the Sydney Morning Herald.

the front page. When they withdraw it, it'll be a tiny blurb that you'll need a microscope to find, on page seven." I was determined to make sure everyone knew that our name had been cleared so that we could start rebuilding the public trust that this investigation had shattered, and so we bought ads in all the papers, with a big bold NOT GUILTY as the headline.

I was more than happy to conclude this saga, but the story was far from over. Though the ACCC's allegations of price fixing were unfounded, there were other troubles within the company that I'd have to deal with in full now that the drama was done. The biggest fire had been put out; it was time to address the many small fires that had been burning slowly for years.

When embarking on such a daunting task, it's easy to get discouraged or overwhelmed. I had been brought in to launch a massive campaign to get Caltex's house in order, and I knew what I was in for when I'd agreed to the job. That didn't make it any less intimidating, but I am not one to give up on something once I've committed to it. Though the details of the strategy will be different depending on your venture, the overarching approach is the same, and it's really not all that complicated. First and foremost, no matter how far you or your company have fallen, you have to remember that it's not enough to simply climb your way out of the hole—you must set the bar as high as it can possibly go, then do what it takes to not only meet it but beat it. Here's how.

DON'T COMPROMISE YOUR PRINCIPLES

Thirty years before this incident, in 1971, Jan and I had decided to change our visit to Mumbai, India to a permanent move for the job at Fiberglass Pilkington Ltd. We had used the savings she'd squirreled away from her paychecks from the University of Washington's housing office to buy appliances and modify them for usage in India. While we were dating, Jan had introduced me to American music, and by that time we had a small collection of LPs—including a few albums from my favorite musician, Neil Diamond—that I wanted to keep, along with Jan's mother's dishes and some other household goods. On our trip back to Seattle to pack up our belongings before the move, we'd traded in Jan's old car for a Volkswagen station wagon, which we took to the port to have shipped. Then we said goodbye.

We cleared all our household goods at customs in Mumbai. All, that is, except the car. It had arrived but, according to the customs officer, we would need to pay a hefty duty on it in order for them to release it from the dock. A couple of trips to Delhi did not solve the issue, and, anyway, I had to start my new job. The car would have to wait.

Then I got a phone call at my new office. The caller did not identify himself. "Your car is stuck in customs," he said.

"Who's this?"

"Don't worry about it," he replied. "I can help you. But I'll need ten thousand rupees from you first."

"Sorry," I said, "I don't do bribes."

Long story short, there was no way we were getting that car back—a car we'd paid good money for and had spent $650 to ship—without greasing some palms, something I was unwilling to do. Following many weeks without progress, we decided to just pay to ship it back to Seattle. Once it arrived, Jan's dad turned the key in the ignition and, when nothing happened, popped the hood. Someone had relieved the car of its engine in Mumbai or during transit.

Looking back, it's clear that this was the first straw of what would eventually break the camel's back. As I noted in chapter 2, India's corrupt bureaucracy was one of the primary reasons we returned to the United States. I could have paid the bribe and been done with it, but I believe that one unethical behavior leads to another, and soon it becomes a slippery slope with no end in sight.

Now, in Australia in 2002, I knew that I needed to pay attention to ethics violations, both egregious and trivial. As was my usual practice, I ordered an audit of the expense reports for all my direct reports, hoping to get a glimpse into their characters. All were squeaky clean, with the exception of one. There weren't always red flags, but the lesser matters—the yellow and orange flags, if you will—were important to me, too. Soon my direct reports figured out that they wouldn't be able to get away with even tiny transgressions, not that most of them were so inclined. They also learned about one of my quirks, which had solidified during those four years in India decades earlier. Indians are known for never showing up on time, and to this day, I have one pet peeve that ranks above all others: being late. (For more on shattering stereotypes about minorities, see chapter 3.) I will always be on time, and I expect the same from everyone I am in contact with, whether they are a family member, a friend, an employee, or the host at a restaurant where I've made a 7:00 p.m. reservation. It's a matter of **treating people with dignity and respect**— if you respect someone, you will not waste their time. To some this might seem trivial, but to me it is a very big deal. So, after one of my direct reports showed up late a few times in a row, at the following meeting I set a basket out on the conference table. "For every minute any one of us comes late," I said sternly to the group, "you must put a dollar in the basket." I looked around at the surprised expressions on their faces. I softened the tone of my voice as I continued, "When there's enough money, we will use it to buy lunch."

My father once told me, "Remember, son, when you work for a company, that institution is enabling you to put food on the table. You must never do anything that will tarnish its image or give it a bad name." His words have guided me throughout my career. My theory is that, if someone makes a small ethics violation that goes unnoticed, they are more likely to do so again and again, until the stakes get bigger and the bad behavior becomes habit. This is true whether you are a mail clerk or the CEO, and it doesn't matter how insignificant a lapse might seem in the moment—you must always **hold yourself and those around you to the highest level of ethics and integrity**, no exceptions.

After rigorous reviews, I was forced to let one of my direct reports go. It was not an easy decision, but I needed to draw a hard line, to show that unethical behavior would not be tolerated. I believe this was a critical step in halting Caltex's downward slide—a company is only as good as the sum of its parts, and by holding each and every individual to the highest standards, we would ensure that the company as a whole was meeting those same standards.

MODEL GOOD BEHAVIOR

At Caltex Australia Ltd, I was dismayed to learn the extent of bad behavior exhibited by a couple of top executives. Apparently, they frequently had long lunches, including several cocktails, followed by naps at their desks. Some had earned reputations for treating subordinates like servants and freely spending on the company's dime. This was not my first experience observing those at the top misusing their power, both in the public eye and behind closed doors.

In 1984, I was sent to Sudan to manage a project involving the construction of an eight-hundred-kilometer pipeline from the Muglad Basin to the Port of Sudan, where the oil would be shipped out to the world market. I planned to scope out the capital city of Khartoum before my family followed, but less than a week after I arrived, rebels shot and killed three of our contractors, and Chevron decided that bringing my family along wouldn't be such a good idea.

With Jan and my young sons safely far away in Oakland, California, my team and I began surveying the area for development. We left the city and headed into the desert, where there was nothing but sand as far as the eye could see, with temperatures reaching 125 degrees Fahrenheit before 9:00 a.m. During the day, we rested in our air-conditioned tent and avoided the hostile sunshine; we worked for a few hurried hours in the early morning and in the evening when the sun was low and the air was at its coolest. It was there that I first saw a mirage, the heat waves shimmering above the white sand in a perfect imitation of water.

For a bunch of engineers and contractors used to busy schedules, these long stretches of inactivity were hard to take. Back in Khartoum, some senior executives had figured out a way to pass the time. They'd managed to smuggle in distillation equipment, which they placed in their bathrooms and used to make a variety of alcohols. It was in one of these converted bathrooms that I had my first test of conscience.

Sudan had just introduced Sharia law, making alcohol production and consumption illegal. Many other activities my colleagues and I would view as benign were now punishable by what we considered to be extreme methods of violence. There was a sharp divide between men and women, those in power and those in service roles. For example, you could not pick up a woman whose car had broken down on the side of the road without the risk of getting convicted of attempted adultery, and if a boss accused his employee of stealing, there would be no due process. Cross-limb amputation—in which an arm and a leg from opposite sides of the body are removed—was a common punishment for even a minor offense, and every so often we'd hear of a woman being stoned to death while her family, claiming disgrace, looked on.

I have personal views on the violent enforcement of Sharia law, but I am not an expert and so will not attempt to explain them here. All this to say that the definitions of moral behavior depend on who's defining them, and people tend to disagree on what's right and what's wrong, regardless of whatever laws happen to be on the books at the time. I was horrified by the cross-limb amputations occurring in the town square, but I was not in a position to protest. It was dangerous for us, as demonstrated by the murder of those three contractors right after our arrival, and though I wasn't afraid all the time—I was able to block it out and focus on my work—I knew how precarious our standing was in that country.

In a post-prohibition United States, a do-it-yourself distillery wouldn't hold any serious criminal risk—or certainly not of the life-and-limb kind—or moral weight. But in Sudan, where alcohol was banned, these senior executives were not only acting foolishly by making bathtub gin, they were putting all of us at risk. There was the usual danger—in fact, a senior engineer had gotten in a car accident while driving drunk, killing one of his passengers and severely injuring the other, who had to be airlifted to a hospital in Nairobi, Kenya, for emergency surgery. On top of that, there was additional danger because they were breaking Sharia law.

When those senior executives showed me their distillery operations, I saw two primary choices in front of me. I could go along with it, in the hopes that I would be accepted into their ranks. The possibility of belonging to a social group, especially for someone who is familiar with being an outsider, is a strong motivator. For a moment I considered it. I reminded myself that, as foreign workers, we had certain perks and exemptions, and so it probably wouldn't be all that big a deal if we got caught. On the other hand, relying on this privilege would be a misuse of power. I knew how terribly easy it was for those without power to get the full wrath of the law, whether they deserved it or not. A few weeks earlier, I'd heard a story about a local housepainter who'd been hired to work on the foreign workers' compound. After he finished the job, he approached the foreman to tell him that there was a little paint left over. "If I leave it, it will dry up," he'd said. "Can I take it home?" The foreman gave his permission, but as the painter was leaving, he was apprehended, accused of stealing, and dragged off to the town square. There, the police immediately amputated his right arm and left leg. All for a few drops of paint at the bottom of the can! Recalling that terrible injustice added a new dimension to this decision about the distillery, making its implications more profound than if the "crime" were taken at face value. If people in our service had to follow the law to its letter or risk dismemberment, we should not treat the law so frivolously.

And so I pointed out to my colleagues that they were guests in this country, and that we should be following its laws. I didn't say what I was thinking: that their actions were stupid and reckless, and that, as senior people within the company, they were setting a terrible example.

During my career, I am happy to say, I didn't work with many senior people who engaged in behaviors that were unethical or illegal, or who lied or cheated or treated their staff like dirt. Of course, there were a few, and because they were outliers they stand out in my memory. Most of those people ruled by fear, because they certainly weren't leading by example or ruling with love or creating an atmosphere that encouraged creativity and self-direction. If you are a leader, or you aspire to be a leader, then you have to model the kind of behavior you expect from your team, both inside and outside the office and during and beyond working hours. As the leader, you have the essential duty of setting the tone—if you are flouting the rules, why wouldn't your subordinates do the same? Holding high standards starts with you.

You might have heard the following advice from parents or teachers back when you were in high school. It applies just as much today.

- Don't succumb to peer pressure. Just because your colleagues are doing something—for example, distilling alcohol in company housing, taking three-hour coffee breaks, or fudging expense reports—doesn't make it OK.
- Always make the ethical choice. Even one small lapse can come back to bite you, and if it doesn't, you will still have to live with it. It's hard work maintaining the cognitive dissonance of demanding ethical behavior from others while not acting ethically yourself.

Explicitly state your expectations around ethical behavior. If employees understand your stance from the start, they will have no excuse for making errors in judgment.

ACKNOWLEDGE PEOPLE'S CONCERNS AND LISTEN WITH EMPATHY

With what had been going on at the top of Caltex, I was not surprised to discover that overall morale was terrible—the worst I'd ever seen. With the prospect of bankruptcy looming, employees were jumping ship left and right. I remember one afternoon, soon after I arrived, when a fire alarm went off in the building. It was past 3:00 p.m. when the fire department finally gave us the all clear; by the time 3:40 p.m. rolled around I started to notice how empty the halls outside my office were. I approached my chief counsel and said, "Helen, where is everyone?"

"This is Australia, Jeet. They're all in the pub," she replied, shrugging. "They're not coming back."

I knew that I would have to do something.

After we posted the NOT GUILTY headlines in every newspaper in the country, I held town halls in every single Caltex location across Australia. In the first one, at the Sydney location, I said, "**I am here to serve you**, the employees of Caltex. I will partner with you, and we will do the right things to turn this business around."

I meant it. But words would not be enough—everyone at Caltex would need to see me fighting for the company, to know that I truly had their best interests at heart.

We began a campaign of cutting costs, improving plant reliability, meeting customer expectations, and partnering with our franchises. Within a few months of my arrival, the union's contract came up for negotiation. The union was known for being militant, and never in Caltex's history had there been a year without a union strike that shut down the plant for at least a couple of days. The leadership team told me that the labor relations manager and external legal counsel would help to negotiate the contract. They had one meeting, after which they reported the lack of progress and said to me, "Those SOBs can't be trusted."

"How about I have a meeting with the union leader?" I said. They stared at me for a moment, saying nothing.

Finally, the external legal counsel said, "We don't want the CEO to be in the same room with them. Their heads will swell and then their demands will go up and we'll never get this thing done." I was not to be dissuaded, and a couple of days later I brought the idea up again. "That would be a huge mistake," they repeated.

"I will meet them," I said, losing my patience. "Please arrange a meeting." The next day, they returned and told me that they'd arranged a fifteen-minute meeting at the refinery. "No," I told them, "I want to have one hour for tea and snacks and one hour for the meeting."

"You are making the biggest mistake of your life," they said, shaking their heads. "You'll regret it. And you're going to make our lives so much more difficult."

"Maybe," I replied, "but that is what I want to do." I ended up sitting down for a cup of tea and a snack with every single labor leader. "I want to work with you," I told each of them in turn. "We need to make this work—for you, for me, for Caltex, for Australia."

"Listen," they said in various ways, "your labor relations guy and lawyer treat us like dogs, like nobodies. We just can't get anywhere with them."

"OK," I said again and again. "I hear you. What can we do to fix this?"

Previously, the negotiations had been high-stakes haggling, with distrust and resentment built up on both sides. They had skipped the most important part—breaking bread and establishing trust. Our meetings over tea were an effort at diplomacy, or what I like to call "tea-plomacy": to roll back bad faith and instill a sense of shared interest and mutual respect. I truly listened to their complaints, misgivings, and, eventually, their demands for the people in their charge. We stopped seeing one another as adversaries and instead began to see one another as part of a team. With the union leaders' feedback ringing in my ears, we changed strategies, and the general manager of operations—who had a good relationship with the union—took over the negotiation. We vowed to do things differently this time around.

That was the first year we reached an agreement without a strike. (And the head of the union and his wife became good friends with me and Jan. They visited us for a few days in California a few years after we returned from Sydney.)

I believe that this was possible simply because their concerns were acknowledged and their voices were listened to with empathy. When stakes are high and the stakeholders are many, it's easy for a negotiation to turn into a war. To avoid that, you must sit down with people, see their faces and learn their names, because when you put a face and name to the individuals with whom you're negotiating, it's easier to recognize their humanity, and for them to recognize yours. Then that war turns into a project, one which you can work on together.

Good leadership starts with an invitation to share a pot of tea, the simplest yet most enduring gesture of goodwill I've ever come across. In my experience, this is the best method for establishing trust, an essential for any working relationship. It also softens the hierarchy, creating a more side-by-side style of exchange that goes a long way toward fostering healthy communication and cooperation.

Of course, positioning yourself on an even plane with your colleagues and peers means you are opening yourself up to the same kind of scrutiny you are giving them. This is a good thing—unless you believe you should be exempt from the rules that apply to everyone else.

If, however, you think that everyone should be held to the same high standards, then operating on an even plane is preferable. Leadership is simply the golden rule writ large: do as you would ask others do.

CHAPTER 8

CREATE A SENSE OF BELONGING

Hurricane Katrina hit the Florida coast on August 25, 2005, then headed west toward the Gulf of Mexico. There it picked up momentum, going from a Category 1 hurricane to a Category 5. By the time it reached the Louisiana coast, it was a Category 3, with winds over 125 miles per hour. It continued its devastation northeast to Mississippi, hitting Jackson County on August 29.

More than 1,500 New Orleanians died from drowning or related injuries after the levees broke and the ocean overtook the city. There were many fewer casualties in the small town of Pascagoula, Mississippi—where Chevron's refinery is located—though the state did sustain more than two hundred deaths. It was a terrible calamity for the whole region and, before the winds had died, the Louisiana National Guard and other local governmental and nongovernmental organizations, along with the United States Coast Guard and the Federal Emergency Management Agency (FEMA), were organizing massive relief operations. On August 30, Chevron's chairman arranged for me to fly out in the company jet to join him for a visit to the area.

Jeet escorting President Bush after Hurricane Katrina
through Chevron refinery in Pascagoula, Mississippi.

There I saw more devastation than I had ever witnessed in my life. From the air, I could see the bare-brick outlines of homes along the beach, as if someone had just poured the foundations, and houses farther inland that had been reduced to jumbles of timber. There were entire rooftops on roadsides, staircases leading up to nothing, and mountains of waterlogged debris. The flooding left some apartment buildings' upper floors and supporting structures intact while washing away the lower floors. Refrigerators, giant trees, power poles, and automobiles were strewn about, along with the smaller household goods and cherished mementos that the surges had dragged out of homes and deposited in piles along washed-out roads.

Later I learned that nearly all of the town's residences had flooded and, once on land, I noticed the ragged-looking chickens walking around—the town's poultry farms and private chicken coops had been dismantled. The refinery itself got hit with twenty feet of water. I'd already been sent some photos of the interiors of employees' homes where the water was still chest-deep. I didn't need to be told that the town didn't have power or potable water or fuel—the breadth of the devastation made that perfectly clear.

Roland Kell, the general manager of the Chevron Pascagoula Refinery, met me at the airport. He'd already begun relief efforts for the employees in his care. With my senior advisor, Mike E. Coyle, human resources manager Greg Wagner, and procurement manager Paul Massih, we set about getting the town back on its feet. We decided that we couldn't wait for FEMA to reach this small town—with such widespread devastation, they had enough on their hands.

The safety and welfare of the employees and their families was top priority. Every day, we would ask Roland, "What do you need today?" and whatever he told us, we did. First, we assigned one of our maintenance crews to repair the city's water treatment plant, and another one to organize cleanup efforts. We brought in well over a hundred diesel generator units and enough trailers for a thousand people, all charged to the company card. For a child who suffered from asthma, we put up a trailer with filtered air, and we flew in doctors from San Francisco to tend to injuries and make sure everyone had proper vaccinations and a supply of their medications. Banks and ATMs were closed, so Greg brought down a large sum of cash, which he handed out to employees so they could buy what they needed. We trucked in gallons and gallons of water from other states, dispensed fuel to city vehicles free of charge, brought in caterers to feed the entire tent city, and shipped in cots and fresh linens so that people could sleep comfortably. Several of our maintenance crews, along with crews from the local construction companies, went around to the city's residences to strip sheetrock and use generators for giant fans to dry out the homes' interiors—without which mildew could set in and what remained of the homes would have to be destroyed. Even retired NBA basketball star Karl Malone came down, with his company's logging equipment and crew, to clean up debris. All of this work was done free of charge.

It's true what they say about crises bringing out the best in people. I heard some amazing stories as I toured the tent city—stories of people, their homes flooded to the second level, climbing onto their roofs to escape, then swimming to safety before getting into boats and paddling door to door to rescue others who were stranded.

On my wall at home, there's a framed newspaper clipping with a photo of me walking with President George W. Bush, who toured the areas hit by Hurricane Katrina. You can see my safety badge, secured on my waistband, with a photo facing out. In it are two of my grand-daughters—my other grandchildren had yet to arrive. They were my reason for being safe. As I met with Chevron employees and their families in Pascagoula, I thought about those two little girls living safely in nearby Texas, their home intact. Every encounter served to remind me that each of us have people we love, and people we would do anything to protect. I did not know most of these employees' histories, their family trees, or even their names, but I knew that we all wanted the same thing: to rebuild their community.

What I keep coming back to, during the course of my career and then while working on this book, is how every day brings incredible complexity and, at the same time, everything always comes down to a few simple things. First, safety must always be the top priority because, obviously, without it you have nothing. Second, regardless of race, gender, or creed, everyone wants to feel like they belong. And third, a company *is* its people, and a company will only thrive if its people are thriving and feel as though they belong. As a leader or aspiring leader, no matter the field, I encourage you to continually remind yourself of these three things, and to chart your course of action using them as your guiding lights. So how can you create a sense of belonging?

INVEST IN YOUR EMPLOYEES AND THEY WILL INVEST IN YOU

I can credit how we at Chevron handled the Hurricane Katrina disaster with the work we did at Caltex Australia Ltd years earlier. During my tenure there, I was asked to speak at a business meeting with corporate leaders in Sydney. It was during the writing of that speech that I developed the concept of a Sense of Belonging and the Sense of Belonging Index, which eventually became the SOB Survey, a questionnaire designed to track employee satisfaction. As I noted in chapter 7, when I first arrived the morale of the employees at Caltex Australia Ltd was terrible, and I wanted to not only demonstrate that leadership cared about their productivity and performance, but about their well-being and sense of belonging, too. We would need to see if the employees understood and bought in to the company's overall vision and mission, if they had productive dialogues with their supervisors and a supportive environment for learning and improving, if they were recognized and rewarded for their work and saw opportunities for professional growth, and if they were able to maintain a healthy balance between their jobs and the other important parts of their lives. Of course, because we are a bunch of metrics-minded engineers, we needed to have data around whether or not the actions we were taking were having an effect.

Though particularly useful during times of transition, in which interpersonal tension and general stress are prone to be higher, these fifteen questions can be used during periods of calm as well. (You should feel free to add other relevant questions that make sense to your organization.) Rather than implementing the SOB Survey as a one-time assessment, use it as an ongoing quarterly or semiannual check-in—with greater frequency in times of instability—to track improvement or regression. You will notice that the SOB Survey doesn't have an odd number of options because, when given the chance, people tend to default to the middle, "neutral" choice—the only way to make a real assessment is to compel real answers.

SENSE OF BELONGING SURVEY

Please use the following scale and mark each question with a number to rate your sense of belonging:

1 = Strongly Disagree   **2** = Disagree   **3** = Agree   **4** = Strongly Agree

1. Are the organization's vision, mission, and values clear?
2. Do you see how your role fits into the vision, mission, and values?
3. Does your supervisor provide clear direction and explanation?
4. Do you receive regular, timely feedback?
5. Do you receive recognition on an ongoing basis?
6. Do you believe you are being recognized and rewarded for your contributions?
7. Does your supervisor encourage teamwork?
8. Does your organization excel as a corporate citizen?
9. Do you look forward to coming to work?
10. Do you see opportunity for advancement?
11. Are you given challenging work assignments that offer professional growth for you?
12. Do you enjoy working with your subordinates, peers, and supervisor?
13. Do you enjoy appropriate work and life balance?
14. Do you have mentors who guide you?
15. Does your organization believe in diversity and inclusiveness?

Obviously, we didn't use the SOB survey in the midst of cleaning up a hurricane, when we were more concerned about whether people had food in their bellies and dry socks on their feet. But it was in the back of my mind as I saw how determined the Chevron employees were to not only rebuild their community but get the refinery up and running. By the time we got it back online, we'd spent tens of millions of dollars on repairs. Still, we gave each and every employee a few extra thousand dollars to help them get their homes in order—to show that we were invested in them. They'd showed us how much they were invested, too.

ASK FOR HELP WHEN YOU NEED IT AND GIVE HELP WHEN ASKED

When I first arrived in the United States, in 1969, there were a number of ways in which I had to adjust to my new country. There were the larger social and cultural issues—the anti-war protests on campus, the more casual style of coed interaction—the cold and rainy weather, the Pacific Northwest English, and all the other great and small things that were different from my native land. And, on a microscopic level, there was the simple fact of being suddenly thrown into a whole new microbiome. This proved challenging for my immune system, and, soon after my arrival, I fell sick with what these days people call "the flu" but back then was simply called "being sick." I had a fever and body aches, and just felt generally and overwhelmingly terrible. My seven roommates brought me hot tea and soup, but otherwise there was little they could do for me, and they had their own adjustments to attend to.

I did not know about the medical services available to all students at the University of Washington, and I probably wouldn't have been able to get to the health center even if I had. So, in my feverish state, I simply took the Yellow Pages phone book, opened it to the pages of doctors' listings, and looked for an Indian-sounding name. Dr. Ahluwalia was the first one I came upon.

I called the doctor and explained to him, in Hindi, that I was fresh off the plane, sick, and didn't know what to do. "OK," he replied, "I will come by this evening to examine you." Later, after he arrived as planned, he gave me some medicine and told me to drink lots of fluids and stay in bed.

"What do I owe you?" I asked as he was leaving.

"Don't worry about it," he replied.

That would have been enough. But, once I was well, Dr. Ahluwalia introduced me to the small local Sikh community that gathered weekly at a house to read from the holy book. He would help Jan and me find a Sikh priest in Canada for our wedding a couple of years later. I have never forgotten his kindness. He went above and beyond the call of duty as a physician, both in the moment when treating me as his patient and later, when he welcomed me into his community. To this day, I think back on him with gratitude.

I met Ms. Huma Abbasi many years later, at the end of 2003. I'd just returned from Australia, ready to take on my new role as president of Chevron global manufacturing. As part of a companywide effort, I was traveling around the globe to do the same kind of town hall meetings that had been so helpful in improving morale at Caltex. Chevron was in transformation, and I needed to explore options around closing certain offices but retaining their best employees. During that tour, I went to Dubai, where I conducted a town hall meeting, followed by the usual Q&A session. Afterward, I asked the head of business, "Among your people, are there one or two whom you'd like us to consider for positions in California?"

Huma Abbasi had asked some thoughtful questions earlier that day, and so I wasn't surprised when he immediately endorsed her. "She'd fit in well in your new Health, Environment, and Safety team," he said.

Huma had a medical degree from Pakistan, and she'd already been handling safety and health for the Dubai region, so her skill set and experience did seem like a good fit. After a couple of conversations on the phone, I offered her the job. She accepted.

Huma moved to California a few months later to begin work in my Health, Environment, and Safety (HES) team. Right from the start she performed well, and I had no qualms about her adapting to her new responsibilities. I did, however, worry that, as a single Pakistani Muslim woman without any family nearby, she might face challenges similar to those I had faced as a new immigrant, or worse, that, since this was just a couple of years after 9/11, she—as a Muslim—would be viewed with suspicion. (I am sorry to say that this continues to be the case.) Even though Huma did not report to me directly, I went out of my way to stay in touch. By this time, the culture at Chevron was changing, and doors were much more open to women and minorities than they had been before. (For more on diversity and inclusion, see chapter 3.) Still, entrance into the leadership pipeline isn't always obvious, particularly for people who are coming in from the outside, and I wanted her to understand the path forward so she wouldn't get lost. Today she is general manager, Global Health and Medical, for Chevron Corporation.

I have two wonderful sons but no daughters, and perhaps that was why I went out of my way to welcome her and, later, to keep tabs on her to make sure she was OK. More likely, I saw a younger version of myself in her—a foreigner alone and new to this country. We had many conversations relevant to our work, and beyond that Jan and I invited her over for dinner many times, and she invited us to her place a few times for a home-cooked meal.

One day out of the blue in 2007, Huma called me up. "I've met someone," she told me, a smile in her voice. "We are getting married."

"Congratulations!" I said. "Who's the lucky guy?" She'd met Larry at Chevron, she told me, and they would be having the Muslim ceremony of *nikah* at a nearby Mosque. I inferred that he was a Caucasian, and I wondered if her parents would have the same reservations that my parents had about their child marrying outside of the faith.

"That's great news," I said. "When will your family be coming in from Pakistan?"

After a pause, she said, "My father's health is not good, and the political situation there isn't good either. No one from my side is going to be able to come."

"This is the biggest day of your life!" I said. For a moment I considered my and Jan's wedding, which my own family had been unable to attend. My good friend, Dr. Rajendar Dev Verma, had stood in. "Huma?" I cleared my throat. "Would you mind if Jan and I stand in for your parents?"

"Jeet," she said. "That would be wonderful."

I hesitated for a moment, knowing that we would have to clear up two issues before moving ahead with this plan. Indian national independence and the delineation of borders had caused significant tension between Sikhs, Muslims, and Hindus in the Punjab region, along the newly created border between India and Pakistan. In the years after India won its independence in 1947, blood had been shed on all sides, with Muslims slaughtering Sikhs and Sikhs slaughtering Muslims. Some members of these groups to which Huma and I belonged still carried anger toward and distrust of the other. Unfortunately, multigenerational feuding, based on conflicts that had occurred a few decades or thousands of years earlier, seems to be the norm all across the globe.

"You need to talk with your parents to make sure it's OK with them," I said. "And I think you will need to ask the imam if he will allow a Sikh into his mosque."

It turned out that Huma's parents were not only pleased but grateful, and the imam had no reservations about welcoming a Sikh man and a white woman, along with the white groom and his family. Huma ordered traditional men's attire for me from Pakistan to wear at the *nikah*, and Jan hosted the henna ceremony at our house for Huma and her bridal party. After the wedding, we had all of the guests over to our house for the reception.

I believe that a good leader creates a sense of belonging, both within and beyond the workplace. In 1985, the year I worked in Wyoming, I asked a draftsman to write my favorite quote in fancy lettering on high-quality stationery, which I then had framed and hung behind my desk. For the next twenty-five years, this quote followed me from office to office, across the world and back. It read, "Success follows when people come first."

This is true for everyone, no matter where you live or work. A motivated employee will take initiative in their job and assist their colleagues, an ambitious businessperson will attend networking events to expand their professional network and make introductions between associates, a sociable person will organize dinner parties with friends and lend their neighbors a cup of sugar, and a family-oriented person will drive their kids to gymnastics practice and travel to a cousin's wedding or a niece's quinceañera. A leader will do all of the above and then some, without drawing distinct lines between the categories of business associate, friend, and family. I don't have a prescription for how you should go above and beyond to show you care to the people around you—it's up to you to navigate the particular expectations and etiquette within your life's spheres. I can tell you this: creating a sense of belonging is more than a nine-to-five job.

CHAPTER 9

CONCLUSION

Like many people, I spent the better part of my life climbing the corporate ladder. I wanted to get to the top, to attain both the status and the responsibility, as well as the challenge and the reward. The shining gold symbol of my early success, the 1985 Mercedes 300SD, was just the first of many possessions that, to me, proved how far I'd come. The pride I felt when driving it off the parking lot was a feeling I chased for the rest of my career.

Each and every acquisition after that required me to constantly outperform my peers. Usually I was judged by both the quality and the quantity of my output and by the sheer hours I spent on company business—and I judged others using the same rubric. Of course, Chevron was in no way the exception when it came to workplace pressure. Everywhere was—and still is—the relentless expectation to do more and to do so with fewer resources and to demand more from one another and ourselves. For both women and men, the ambition to "have it all" means overburdened schedules that require maintaining a frenetic pace, in which checking email at the dinner table, having to choose between completing a presentation or tucking a child in to bed, or skipping a fitness class to take a conference call are standard practices.

Jeet and Jan enjoying retirement.

I'll admit that I readily participated in the culture of busyness, even giving compliments disguised as admonitions to subordinates who had sent middle-of-the-night emails. *That's dedication,* was our thinking and we often recognized and rewarded it as a contribution to the company's success. Never did I question whether a human being can actually consistently produce high-quality work and make high-quality decisions if they are putting in eighteen or twenty hours a day. I had done the same, after all, and this mode of operation was the only one that I knew. In fact, I remember often making statements like, "I can get it done, but I wish there were thirty-two hours in the day."

The very first time I stopped to think about this state of affairs was when I spent three days at The Human Performance Institute (HPI) in Orlando, Florida, in 2008. Chevron had sponsored me, with the idea of sending me as a guinea pig to try out HPI's corporate athlete training. Looking back, it's clear that they made a mistake.

Cofounded by Dr. Jim Loehr and Dr. Jack Groppel, the fundamental assumption at HPI was that human beings are fully integrated, multidimensional energy systems, and that true corporate athletes are able to manage pressure at work, manage their time efficiently, tap into their intellect on demand to make critical decisions, deliver superior performance, and maintain a balance between work and family. HPI focuses on managing *energy*, not managing time, using the sciences of performance psychology, exercise physiology, and nutrition. Their **common-sense principles** are:

- Energy, not time, is the fundamental currency of high performance. It is not the amount of time you invest that drives success, but rather the energy you bring to the time you invest.
- Deepening employee engagement is essentially an energy-management challenge, and assessment should be based on health and happiness as well as performance.
- There are four kinds of energy—physical, emotional, mental, and spiritual—and the reservoirs of energy are *not* bottomless.
- Managing energy is an acquired skill set that can be enhanced through training in much the same way that skills for managing time and money can be cultivated.

I'd known at some level that, when overworked, we suffer from fatigue that compromises our ability to fully engage with family and loved ones, and that we sacrifice health and happiness in order to meet the excessive demands and pressures at work. I'd accepted this as par for the course—the toll you must pay to provide. Like many executives, I believed my purpose was to be the best, to win, and to prove my worth through accomplishment. It wasn't really until the corporate athlete training that I realized just how obsessed I had been with success, some of which was motivated by my desire to show the world that an Indian American could perform not just as well as but *better* than anyone else. I used the relative poverty of my youth to justify my oversize drive by telling myself, "I want my kids and grandkids to have anything and everything that I could not have growing up." In no way did I regret making my sons' and grandchildren's lives easier through the comfort and access that money creates; what I regretted was the long hours I spent at work and away from my boys, my absence on weekends and holidays. I regretted using my patience up at work so that, by the time I got home, I had little left for my wife. I regretted snapping at my aging father when, out of worry, he asked me questions more than once. I regretted all those times I checked and rechecked my phone for messages while I was with my granddaughters.

At sixty-two years old, I realized that it might be time to make a big change. I had accomplished material and professional success, more than I could have imagined when I set out to explore this great land of opportunity. What did I have left to prove? During a quiet moment of reflection, the answer came to me: nothing.

I wonder what my life would have been like if I'd attended the Human Potential Institute earlier. Would I have conducted myself differently? Would I have reached the same level at Chevron? Would I have been healthier or happier? Would I have been more engaged with the people I love?

For these questions I have no answer. But I believe it's never too late.

And so I retired from Chevron the following year, in 2009. My third granddaughter, Kylie, was two years old, and my fourth granddaughter, Lucy, had just arrived. Lucy was born in Russia in 2009 and adopted by my son Amby and his wife, Jenny, in 2012, just before her third birthday.

At the time of this writing, on February 5, 2019, we welcomed our charming and handsome grandson, Frankie. These days, I still spend a significant part of my life traveling and in board meetings in far-flung locales, but I also spend more time dedicating myself to my health, my family, and my community. I go for walks every day, and sit with a cup of tea and no other distractions. When I visit my grandkids, I put the phone aside. I do what I can to show my wife how lucky I feel for getting to spend the last nearly fifty years with her. And I give back to the organizations and communities that helped my own rise, like the University of Washington—the institution that brought me to America—and the town in India where I grew up. Though Shri Joshi, my blind tutor who first showed me what it means to love learning, is no longer living, his grandchildren are—and to them I've tried to express my thanks.

It's never too late to examine your life and make adjustments. We all have only so much time on this earth, and only so much energy. What and who are your top priorities? To the people and projects that matter the most, give only your best. You can let circumstances drive your life, or you can create the circumstances that bring joy to your life. The choice is yours.

Bindra grandkids (ages) L to R: Kylie (12), Lily (15), in
lap Frankie (6 weeks), Gracie (13) and Lucy (9)

LEADERSHIP PRINCIPLES

1. Believe in "I'm possible" instead of "impossible"
2. Advocate for yourself
3. Establish a track record
4. Believe that you have a choice
5. Find a mentor
6. Hold high standards
7. Remember people's names and maintain relationships
8. Treat others as they would like to be treated
9. Judge people by their behavior
10. Give people a second chance
11. Always be on time
12. Join the mainstream
13. Advocate for diversity plans
14. Broaden your network
15. Treat others with dignity and respect
16. Be flexible
17. Say "Thank you"
18. Be adventurous
19. Seize every opportunity

20. Don't procrastinate

21. Make decisions using the 80/20 rule

22. Know where the pressure is coming from

23. Say "I serve you"

24. Disrupt thinking

25. Admit vulnerability

26. Maintain humility

27. Make fun of yourself

28. Provide direction

29. Steward business

30. Get over failure

31. Accept interpersonal differences

32. Empower and develop people

33. Acknowledge people's concerns

34. Celebrate successes

35. Recognize and reward excellence

36. Take a stand against injustice, prejudice, and discrimination

37. Create a Sense of Belonging (SOB)

38. Perform daily assessment

39. Prepare for negotiation

40. Be a mentor

41. Give lots of feedback (positive and negative)

42. Let go through delegating

43. Listen with empathy

44. Take things one day at a time

45. Share the limelight

46. Focus on what's important

47. Communicate, communicate, communicate

48. Establish a business case for change before implementing changes; explain what's not changing

49. Engage not only the minds but also the hearts of the team members

50. Benchmark against the best (never compare your performance against the industry average)

51. Use every interaction with employees to reinforce incident- and injury-free principles and behaviors

52. Catch people doing things right and reinforce

53. Reward differentially

54. Use diversity as a competitive advantage

55. Maintain the highest level of ethics and integrity

56. Hold people accountable

57. Reinforce right behaviors even if you disagree with the content

ACKNOWLEDGMENTS

I wish to thank everyone who helped me achieve this dream of writing a book.

Thank you to Chuck Gibbs, my executive coach at Chevron. You believed in this book from day one. Your encouragement and our intensive brainstorming helped launch this project.

Thank you to my colleagues at Chevron. Shariq Yosufzai, Jane Doty MacKenzie, Huma Abbasi, Mike Coyle, Bruce Chinn, and Greg Wagner, I greatly appreciate you contributing your time, expertise, and memories. I am proud to call you my friends.

Amy Maki, you have been a dear friend to me and Jan for more than fifty years, and you know our long history better than almost anyone. Thank you for recalling student days gone by.

A big thank-you to my editorial team. Anna Katz, thank you for truly listening to me and capturing both what I was saying and what I was trying to say. Your outstanding work was essential to this project. Girl Friday Productions, thank you for your guidance in and dedication to turning an idea into a reality. Thanks to Dave Valencia, Laura Lancaster, and Tanqueray Strange for your editorial contributions, and Micah Schmidt and Rachel Marek for bringing it all together.

Words cannot express my gratitude to my lovely wife, Jan, who has stood by me and given me her unwavering support for all these years. Whatever personal and professional success I have achieved has been earned jointly by the both of us. That success includes our loving, generous, and caring sons, Amby and Shammi, and their lovely brides,

Jenny and Melissa. Our lives are further enriched by our gorgeous and supersmart granddaughters, Lily, Gracie, Kylie, and Lucy. Welcome, Frankie, to the family. You bring smiles to our faces every single day.

ABOUT THE AUTHOR

Jeet S. Bindra was born into modest circumstances in Benares (now Varanasi), India. In 1969, after graduating in chemical engineering from the Indian Institute of Technology, Kanpur (India), he came to the United States as a graduate student at the University of Washington, where he earned a master's degree in chemical engineering. Jeet went on to acquire an MBA (with honors) from Saint Mary's College of California. He began his professional career as a research engineer for Chevron, and over the course of his thirty-two-year career there took on increasing levels of responsibility, eventually retiring as the company's president of global manufacturing.

Jeet has been a tireless advocate of diversity and inclusion throughout his career. He has been a keynote speaker at conferences for the Society of Hispanic Professional Engineers, the Society of Women Engineers, the Society of Black Engineers, as well as the American Society of Engineers of Indian Origin. He has delivered commencement addresses at Cal Poly San Luis Obispo, San Jose State University, as well as his alma mater, the Indian Institute of Technology, Kanpur, India.

During his career, he implemented many new ideas, tools, and practices designed to create a sense of belonging in an organization.

He has also been a catalyst for change, known for leading underperforming organizations to the top end of industry benchmarks.

Jeet has served on the Board of Directors of several publicly listed companies from India to Australia, Europe, and the United States. He has also served as the chairman of the University of Washington, College of Engineering Visiting Committee, and as Distinguished Honorary Professor at the Rajiv Gandhi Institute of Petroleum Technology. Among his many honors are the Diamond Award from the University of Washington College of Engineering and the Distinguished Alumnus award from the Indian Institute of Technology, Kanpur.

Jeet and his wife, Jan, are involved in charitable work for the education of underprivileged boys and girls in India, including establishing an endowed chair as well as a professorship in the Department of Chemical Engineering at the Indian Institute of Technology, Kanpur. They have also endowed an undergraduate scholarship, a graduate fellowship, and a professorship, as well as the Bindra Innovation Laboratory, to the University of Washington.

Jeet and Jan live in Seattle, Washington.